Blockade and Barricade Runners:

The First Door Runners of the French Campaign

By: Caius Homme

Part I

Looking from the table to the crystalline coast, the French diver grinned as her mate scupped with her in the local handout. On the shore, gulls drifted back and forth through the air, and Sebastian smiled as he watched a little blonde love scuttle back and forth on the sea grass and try and catch the gull.

The gulls floated to the air, sailing back and forth, picking up wind in their wings as the sky opened above to a bright blue sky and sea. Dipping her Aussie sticks to the ketchup, the diver bared her teeth with the silliest spout of ketchup dripping from fries.

On her right, an old salty sea sailor grinned and bore his drift eye her way and looked to the pylons of the dock.

"Do you know where my mates be?" he asked.

She looked to the left and cut her eyes to the right at the large marina dock in the distance of the inland sound and put her boot to the edge of the table.

"Ah, by this time, they should be scuttling off to the sound with their flippers and scuba gear," she said.

Her French companion smiled and nodded.

The night before had been a bit of heaven, as the pair sat on the top of the diver's red terrain vehicle by the sand and watched the stars shoot across the sky. There was star light of blue and a few drifting ones of red, and in the afternoon, the French mates wandered through the sidewalks of the coastal town hand in hand.

She had pointed out various corbel and lintel archways of the historic town, and he didn't mind when she showed him the graveyard and pointed out the oldest graves of the sea.

"That one might have been a sailor," she said. "And his bonnie be by the tide."

The crisp cool air of the spring tides always rushed forth with the warm sunlight of the sky and the cool breeze of the drifting air of the mid-Atlantic to the north and the warm sun driven tides of the South seas.

Hand in hand, the diver looked back and forth to the Spanish moss and oaken board of the houses and looked to the Frenchman.

"Perhaps a bit of scup along the sea port with the mariners," she said.

And, hand in hand, the pair wandered with the little petit belle joli on her back to the sea.

Looking to the table, the diver's green eyes stared intense to hers, as if asking, what coastal breeze would be the next boat out. Stepping up from the table, Emerili looked to the next room of the outdoor restaurant and wandered in and out of the people stepping back and forth.

There were young lasses skipping rocks along the old diving ground, and a couple of sea maids lifting napkins from the tables as the mariners wandered in with the fresh catches of the day. On the dock, there were a few tuna, snapper, and sea bass.

Looking down, Emerilli pointed to the line and drag of the old sea boat on the dock that had stopped for a scup.

"What warm waters did you find that in?" she asked.

Lifting his knee to the stern of the ship, he displayed the bright scaled fish and bore his arm with the shipman's ink and drive.

"Ay," he said. "The southern tides are driving in down by Charleston and Savannah."

Nodding, she smiled.

"Well, I know where to head next," she added.

In the restaurant, Emerilii placed a note to the wait table as Brishon lifted it. His green blue eyes pierced hers, and he looked to the back of the restaurant where some of the sea divers instruments were placed.

"The privateers will be headed south in the next week," she said. "Guess you all will be finding a ship or a moat for a bonnie be."

Looking to the scuttle room of the restaurant, the sailors in the port town wandered back and forth lifting plates and dinner bells to the mariners and their birdies and brides-to-be. Emelli smiled and pointed at the harpisonic bell and steel poles plugged in, and laughed.

"You are twittering in the restaurant with that thing," she said, lifting the green harpisonic sound machine.

"What is this supposed to be?" Brishon asked.

"It's a supersonic pulse to accelerate sound waves in the sea or the air," she said. "It calls in fish or collapses sound waves."

"What am I supposed to do with this?" he asked.

"Go call in some fish or I don't know, find your mates and have a bit of fun and shut down the wire and find a girl," she added.

Watching as the sea diver passed through the bathroom and tilted a few mirrors, he smiled and looked to the bright sunshine in the sky. It was no longer orange, but the cool sunlight and breeze of a natural spring sun.

Emerili and the Nacht Ronne

In the night, the lithe brunette lifted foot and foot to the moonlit orb of the sky. The night air wasn't as cold as the day before, and the silent sound of the waves and constant momentum of arms in the sea lifted and fell. In swirls, the black forms drifted in and out of the sea, and Emilii ran.

The air smelled of gunpowder, men and lead, and looking to her moon she lifted foot and foot to the drifts as the sound of line and fire accelerated in the night by the sound.

Pulsing, her heart looked to the sea, and she removed the soft linen of the divers and barrel rolled to the sea. The water no longer hurt and her feet felt as they had in youth, the soft silk of a seal's skin.

As the red tide of clouds rolled from the south across the coastal town, the faint shadows of the air collided with the distant electric storm of the light house and as she cleared another mile of topography, a bolt of lightning shot from the softest silver cloud to the shore.

Accelerating along the coast, Emilii's silver shape could see the house lights of the pier turned on and the smell of sulfurous ions to the air.

The silver and line of the stealth night cast from the cargo hold of the air and the line placed along the shore as the black forms lifted from the sea and collided to the sandy drifts. It was the southern tides returning to find the last swimmers and sails of the sea.

"Is there someone there to reach me, or is there someone there to find me?"

Looking to the salty waves, the black forms retrieved the remaining men of the sea and turned on the yellow and green night lights of the diver team in the night. Emerilii watched as the cast and net lifted from the water to the sky and the last of the black forms returned to the air or ran along the sea coastline.

Emerili looked along the coast and cut to the pavement of the houses. In the night, the jeeps of the renegades parked overnight rode down the shoreline lifting wire and line to make sure everyone was back in safe.

Looking to the moon, the scout wandered to the back yard and arbor of her best mate in town, and began flipping in the dusty soil. From his window, Auduoin smiled as he could hear the light bells of Emilii's heart lift.

"Vaht habe Fraulein?" he asked his sleeping mate, elbowing him awake.

"Fraulein est doing flips in the nacht," he said, grinning, as the rustle of leaves filled the air.

Waking up from the night air, Emerilii had fallen asleep on the deck of the haus, and when she awoke she found little scallops, a few black oyster pearls, and the beautiful diadem and seagrass necklace of a joli belle beside her.

"Il est sept?" Emerilli asked, jumping up.

"J ai," she said, aloud, and lifted from the ground and began packing quietly.

The coastal tide and breeze and bells of the bonnie brides rose to the air, and in the distance, the storm of Provencal rising again to sight.

Waifing through the sound, Brishon looked across the estuary with a fishing pole in hand. The gulls swooped and dived to the eddys along the shore and a small flock of grey gulls gathered at its center. On the dock, Brishon eyed a lithe blonde in cut-off shorts and a dive shirt tying knots.

Wandering to the dock, he spotted sailor knots and a handful of neatly plait sailor bracelets. Grinning, she lifted one to the air and threw it at the fisherman like a snowball. The spring winds rose to the air, and the cold feeling of the water on his boots reminded Brishon of a first kiss in the crisp air of a early Southern tide.

Treading water in the shallow eddy, Brishon searched for the sailor's fist that Eemeril tossed to him. In the murkish water, the sailor knot floated, and he noticed a basket of ten more.

"What have you all been up to love?" Brishon asked.

Emerilii smiled, and lowered her eyes.

"We got word we were in it for a bit of rope tying," she said. "So, we made a plan to get out of it."

"How long have you been here?" he asked looking at the massive amount of rope tying and scout knots.

"Eh, we held this for a long time," she said. "The French Fatale Femme Tactic."

"Oh, yeah?" he asked.

She smiled and handed him a sandwich.

"Yeah, we just made a lot of noise and talked about the worse things that could happen, and they boys finally gave up and ran off somewhere else," she said.

"That's a pretty good tactic, love," he added.

"What did you tell them?"

"Oh, the truth," she said, swiping her lips on her sleeve from the jam sandwich. "That there is a lot of dead around here and what's not dead will kill you."

She pointed to the dark grey clouds on the horizon and a stack of dark green French commodant uniforms hanging on the banister and rail of the old beach house.

"The ones that are visible aren't that bad," she said. "Just the ones that come in the night to collect on what the day ones found."

Chatting about an old sailor tale of how some basic lovers tricked the admiral into playing a love song on the air instead of another war epic, Emerilii joked and placed the basket in his arms. In the night, she and Auduoin spent a couple of hours tying loose knots and bound sailor fists to figure out how to escape the next round of naval torture.

"We are just going to slip these on the ends so everyone gets out real quick, and we don't' get stuck having to do a bunch of training over this," she said, handing a bunch of red slips of paper to the trash.

"Now, go find where he plans to put us, and pick some good mates, and we are just going to joke this scuttle duck right to the bottom of the shore," she said.

In the night, Auduoin drove to the outskirts of town, finding the shouts of time and muffle of gag and bound foot infantry. In the dimming sun, he spotted the small black door of the wood leading to the metal industrial garage by the sea.

Phoning Emilii a du wood,

"Do you see this video?" die kein infantry asked a du ground. "Sous Ja."

"Quelle est it?" he asked.

Pointing to the rock haus at the entrance of the city, she identified the falta haus auf die femmes, and to the rechts she pointed out the disaster relief building that was used for hand-to-hand combatants and in the center by the airfield, the BAL training haus.

"That is used to pick and abduct some of the kids in town for intense firing squad lines and throwing them in a box and driving them around until someone finds them," he said.

"En le noir, ponce du X on that," one said.

"Was know that?" he asked.

"Ich vast there," she said. "Now, quite stopping my damn heartrate or I have to start punching my chest to get it going again."

"Pour quoi?" he asked. Lifting her metal locker from the ground, she lifted out the pedal hand and showed it and the lens of her eye.

"It will pulse it fast and then stop it and then you get processed with a needle in your damn eye," he said.

"Well, then, let's do some ripcord landing then," he said.

The Nacht und Muerte

In the night, the admiral wandered to the garage behind the marina and found seven bound sails and bonnies-to-be. In the night, Roan recalled lifting her feet on the ground, as she watched the others walk in front of her, shuffling feet through the wood.

"Ah, she's not awake one bit during that," a voice whispered to her side.

In the dark room, she spotted a mate in the back sitting with his arms raised, with wrists hanging by the axel of truck and rope on the ground. From the side, a large man walked in.

Sitting, he walked up and jerked Emerilii's head up.

"What in the hell did you sell to the state?" he asked.

She grinned, spitting a tooth to his palm.

"Just a bit of love and a lot of short one-liners," she said.

In her mind, she recalled the joy of Severin's timing on the dryer and the smile spread across the ground like butter on bread, her legs open and wide as the river and sea. His tawny shoulders keeping time with all the father's singing in the house that night.

"Sont du vife," the French door runner said, spitting blood to the floor. "Her voce sang like a turkey goblet."

Angered, the American commodant looked to her pissed as the glint of his gold ring turned black as the night.

"This bitte doesn't shut it," he said.

Sitting in chairs looking at the dim rose light of the night room, the eight Aberdessen of the pilot lifted their hands from the line and drag of the recovery boats as four vert shirts with taunt muscle stepped aside. Uncrossing her legs, she threw down her arms and jerked the American admiral to the air and dropkicked him to the ground with an added curb stomp for the pleasure of his bonnie-to-be.

Walking out, the seven pelted the admiral with the sailor knots he had their bonnie-to-bes make all day so they could go to and scup at the purple fishy restaurant.

Wandering forward after the chum buckets were full, Emerilli lifted her thumbtacks and scattered them across the floor. Removing his deck boots, she grinned and sat a little golden egg with timer to the marina door.

"Loved your egg salad, love," she said.

Walking out and spitting out her mouthpiece, Emerilii jumped up and side poked her mate.

"That wasn't so bad, now, was it," she said.

"How did you know the children's training exercise on knot tying was going to end bad?" Brishon asked.

Emerilii grinned.

"Ah, you know us lonely kids on the block…anything we buy is always used against us," she said.

Sitting down a bottle of homemade wine and a dozen eggs from her farm inland, she lifted her pink scubbing boots and wandered back to the sea with the song of the black night room fading with the ocean sun and scattered ash of the admiral's scubbing floor.

Die Meer

Walking from the ocean, Emerilii stepped to shore and placed a basket of sailor bracelts to the shore and walked from the sea to the shore and to the distance, and disappeared. In the waterway, the stream of lye spread by the recovery boats bled from white to red as she placed the bloody knots to the salt water. And, there was no one.

Brishon walked from the shore and to the beach house concealed within the Cyprus trees. Retrieving a sailor's bracelet, he walked from the sandy dunes to the house. The old pieces of pier that he discovered in the shallow inlet where he had inlay a beautiful carving of the sea while on the mariner's ship smoothed beneath his hands.

Inside, his first mate sat in her long dungarees with her wading boots on. Scubbing on a toast sandwich, she grinned.

"Why are you here in the middle of the day" he asked, placing his scuba flippers to the stool.

She grinned, wiping her lips with her blue thermal.

"Ah, I spotted something that no one understands a le mer," she said.

Pointing to the drawing on the wall, she pressed her feet against the oaken weatherboard countertop and leaned back in the kitchen bar stool. The industrial lamp glowed overhead, and a wind chime played on the front porch.

Casting her eyes back to the gentle lull and ring of the chime, she lifted her sea glass soda pop.

"They didn't know I had a special ship for thunder storms," she laughed, hiccupping.

In the corner, her grey knapsack and pack lay on the floor beside some damp knit beside a silver shell made of a cerulean mollusk.

Jumping up from the bar stool, she stood and slid into her suspenders and lifted her second pair of scubbing boots. Tossing a kiss to the air, she whispered a "Lieben du, schlapen du," and side kicked his tush.

"Lieben du toi, liebe," he replied.

Tapping the sailor's love knot on the glass table with Cyprus tree basin, she smiled.

"Guess ya'll got up a bit late, love," she said. "But, thanks for completing that morning swim for me."

Swimming out past the breakers, Emerilli dove below the water. The silver netting of the carrier and destroyer was nearby, and she slipped below the waves sinking to the bottom, looking for shells and the large whelks of the deep aphotic zone.

From behind, a large sting ray swam near, its humming pulse echoing loudly in her ears.

From the dark green water, a handsome seal in training rose from the water, lifting his topography tent from the water and replaced it back to his pack.

"Quelle, love," he said. "It wasn't a sting ray, it was just my underwater topography tent. It looks like a stingray, but it is just a way for me to maneuver through the sea to the land without being seen."

Taking her hand, he grinned.

"Now, let's roam and run," she said.

Running from the seashore down the coastline, the pair hummed and completed the last set of push-ups on the shoreline. Roan's arms beat to the pulse of fifty, and beside her, the vert eyes of the second runner cut to hers as the shock of the stealth collided to the sea and shore 3 kilometers in the distance.

"Il est diverssante," she said, laughing to the air, pulling him up, and setting a peg to the sand. As I looked to the night, he felt the lift and light air of being carried to the distance, until he felt asleep. Waking from the night to the daylight of the morning sky, the crystalline glass of the sand sparkled with the light of a sunrise in glows of rose, bleu, jaune, and the sea.

Watching her feet lift from the sand, Roan pointed to the sun in the sky and the shot of a reactor pulse to the air.

"Ut, it's okay," she said, "My satellite's reactor was firing too hot and the sun was burning red, so we dipped it to the ocean."

"Now, komme avec moi main," she replied, reaching her hand to his.

"Vaht?" he said pointing to the sea.

"Ah, non, je parlez main et je meant moin," she said, reaching out with her hand.

Along the port town, the pair wandered a few miles, looking to the sea and the distance blue clouds of the deep ocean, and finally the horn and whistle of the boat houses. Standing by the gazebo of the sea as the next naval transport barrage drifted in with a dismantled satellite, Kristalnod and Arya smiled at the little jaune belle laughing and running in front of them with her palms open chasing the gulls.

"A petit belle, vous gull ne aimes quell," Arya said.

Looking back, the stubborn blonde picked up pieces of bark off the ground, chasing the gulls around. Laughing, Arya grinned and pointed out the flock on the gazebo, looking for direction.

With her eye, she whistled and a couple captains walked from the topography and the trio looked right and then left, sending the gulls to scan the topography, the water below, and inland to sound off the joy of the sea to the city.

"They fly on," Arya said, nodding to Kristalnod and the petit cheri.

Sailing in, the barrage of the inland bound gear of the sea arrived to shore.

"Voudrais parle a le capitain pour un satellite rod of that?" she asked, as the circular landing gear of the satellite passed on the barrage to the distant inter coastal waterway.

"Nah, Komme auf," Kristalnod said to Arya.

Wandering to the city, the pair intertwined hands and the sound of the belles giggles filled the air. On the sidewalk, the brick and mortar line of the shipmen sailing to the city lined in cars. Arya looked to the churlish belly and suspender of the city shipmen, and the grave importance of the timing of the barrages arrival.

"Daughters of the state," one whispered to his watch.

Wandering forth on foot and by hand, the beauties of the governor's ball walked through the city streets and supped with the men of the sea. There were ones made of streets of gold with the blonde locks of travel, and there were ones of red with the fiery tongues of the chemists and hounds, and at last, lithe brunettes of a higher order.

"Perhaps you can tame a tongue or two," she whispered, looking to the arriving Escalades and cars in pairs and trios. "Or at least send one in the right direction."

Lifting his arm with the hammer and rod of the Shipman's anchor tattoo, the privateer captain looked over the Arya.

"Do you know what is going on?" he asked, looking to the sea and glancing over to the visible window and nodding. Walking by, a man and woman casually walked, tapping her table on the hand twice.

Eyes widening and alert, Arya smiled, sneering at the lofty thought of being selected.

"It is always this time of year, the colleges release a few to sea to determine a potential pair," Arya said, at lunch, scubbing on some fish from the private deck and ships sailing in. "Now, just donne a bon moin."

At the glass, a shipman lofted to the glass and surveyed the available femmes in the room as the rogue spy dressed as a sea diver continued making a charade of impetuous youth to their face.

Grinning to Kristalnod, she lifted the bottle of red ketchup and squirted it down her throat, laughing, in the casual err and circumstance of a diversion. The eyes of the selection turned to her in grotesque, and in the corner, Henri took the four gems at the door by the hand and led them away.

"Nie, lauf," the sailor said. "Komme meine."

Finishing up, the sailor to her left looked to the little belle of Heaven and cut his eyes down looking away as Arya lifted her pack and wandered back to the city.

When I look in your eyes, I am ahead, and can't grow tired, the shipman and sailor said, smiling.

Door Runners and Hovers

Driving through the city lights of Provencal, the door runner watched the cars line in paired numbers, swirling in line side to side.

"Il est un bon pairing," he said, looking to the lad beside him.

"Donne moi," the gerl in the back said.

The car lined, and passed through the hurry of the city at night, watching the passing bridges circle back and forth, and Kristalnod looked to Arya, her eyes down set and focused.

"Should we teach these to lift, love?" she asked.

He nodded, grinning.

Tuning the radio knob, the pair echoed the sound waves of the hover through the cars and Kristalnod looked to the sky towers in the distance, pulsing light, as Arya's back flexed.

Passing from the right, a truck illuminated with the bright light of the sky towers lifted forward, and the plane of cars drove forward, passing through seventy miles of topography in six seconds.

"Auf, love," Arya smiled, grinning.

The truck towered to the air, its running boards bright with light.

"Whew, auf fast," he said, looking over to the green eyed Wunden beside him.

Looking ahead, the femme door runner watched the pulse and sound of lights collide into one, and she looked to the dark of the night, the mer in the distance.

Returning, Arya woke to the sound of a telephone and the ring of a snow. The ice collided to the streets, and she honked her horn to the cars in front of her as they stopped in the middle of the interstate trying to line up.

"Nie," she said. "Non sont pour convoy…parle a le pilot et ice take off training."

"Vaht?" her car passenger asked, looking alerted and strapping his seatbelt.

Accelerating in the ice on the open highway, the red car slid side to side as Arya gained momentum to grip the tires to the street for take off.

"Shite, suss miche," Severin shouted holding the Gott handle

"Gott handle?" she said, looking ahead as the road climbed.

Accelerating, the bleu lights of the commodants trying to access accidents to the left motioned for her to slow down.

"Nein, Ich bin a airfield," Arya yelled back, cutting to the right and back to the left.

"Wir practicing flight training morgen," she said.

To her right, the blockade runner grinned and continued to hold the Gott handle, eyeing the feisty femme to his left. As they passed the electrical tower of the air field, he watched her pulse the satellite radio to signal the civic patrol to wake up in the snow and prep the air field for training.

"Dietrich, komme auf," Arya shouted aloud. "Nein, Ich nein…Ich kein problem et aujourd'hui, un homme parle pour ice in Mars."

Laughing, she heard the jovenes pilot pick up helmets and step to the airfield as the vieux pilots prepped them for taking off in snow and ice for disaster relief. The sound of the airwaves pulsed again, and Arya continued forward to the city to run the emergency routes.

Beside her, Severin laughed and as she wandered to the light of the market for supply, he turned and asked her why there was ice in the spring.

"Polar landing training pour Alaska," she said, smiling.

Driving off with the nearest Jeep renegade, Severin headed to sea. In his way, the terrible driving of civilians on the road made him remember training in a previous assignment.

"Ich bin blockade runner," he said, flashing his white strobe light to the left.

Crashing forward, he pointed to the renegades with hazard lights to the right.

"Pilot, combat driver?" he asked, picking up a tall Deutsch youth to his Jeep.

"Da, Vader," he said.

"Nie, just Vader Blockade Runner," he said, grinning. "Now, hold on."

Accelerating forward, the blockade runner clicked down his side panels and the pair drove forward, the bumper and crash of the side rail ringing aloud all the way to the mer. Laughing, the pilot clicked his red light.

"Auf du," he said. "Le jovenes kein problem."

Laughing, the honky red light and horn sirens of the fire engines rose to the air and down the streets lifting people from the cars.

"Ich bin clearing the emergency lane," the Deutsch commodant announced aloud. "Wir kommen…. Gott, Du kein problem, Arya?"

"Mach schnell," the pilot shouted, honking his horn, as Severin pressed the brake, tapping his red lights to wake up the two behind him.

"Hurry up, suss miche," one spoke to the other as the trio headed to sea. "Sie kir problem."

"Nie, Ich drove straight, le naval cut through three lanes," the femme commodant shouted over the airwaves, laughing. "Wir zwei weeks of this mess."

Atop the acceleration ramp of the emergency exit, __ girl driver___ spotted the Jeep renegade accelerate forward and for a moment his eyes caught hers in panic.

Driving forth, she cut three lanes over and began laughing.

"Auf du…never met a blockade runner before," she said. "Wir use it and learn from it."

Auf Minefield France

In the late evening, the American renegade convoy accelerated down the dirt road to the secluded encampment by the large open spaces next to le Sur Mer du France. The hum and speed of the renegade collided in the sandy soils of the French chapparel as an artillery convoy parked at its exit. On foot, a small patrol cautiously wandered through the dense wood to survey the campsite.

The nettles and stumps of the pine wood concealed their sound as they lightly coursed through the sandy soil. Walking forward with rifle in hand, the commodant lifted his fist for the artillery squad to move in closer.

Lifting his pack, Russell set down four spools of line, a handful of iron poles, as the convoy retrieved an activation piece from their packs. In the back, six or eight placed large black duffel bags of black cylinders to the ground.

From the side, one drew a map of the area on the dirt and the group broke into pairs to place the line and wire of a minefield. Digging plants with shovels and scattering nettles, the groups set line across seven miles of topography in the dark, as the clouded cover of an aircraft's atmospheric blanket concealed them.

It was 3 a.m. when the first wave of boats began accelerated through the waters. From the sound, Brenden could hear the hum of motor craft in the water. Turning over, he lassoed his arm in his bunkmate, trying to sleep in the house the pair had discovered the night before.

Murmuring in his sleep, his friend made a sound. In the room next door, Sirene eyes shot open and she stood in the dark. She could hear the watercraft and in the distance, the sound of the ocean to her ear. There was no light in the sky or houses on the street, but she looped her street shoes and went for a midnight run.

Behind her, a German runner traveled behind her, and the short, shrill whistle of a bird in air passed to the bridge. In the short flash of her eye, she saw the silver movement of a rifle from the bridge to the cover of the cypress trees below.

As she passed over the bridge, she heard the line and fire of an underwater mine shudder and the short range blast and light of gunfire to the air. It was a sequence of six to seven rifles fired at once. Accelerating to the sea, the sound passed into the rushed wind of the le Meer.

Passing over the waterway, Le Sur Mer rose to sight, and the sand felt damp beneath her feet. Running along the shoreline, she could see the cascading light of the moon on the sea, and the rising arms of swimmers rising and falling into the water. Behind her, the auburn arms of the German runner on foot looked to the shore, surveying the landscape for safety for the second runner.

"Auf a temporary alliance with she," he said, pointing to her form, barrel rolling in die Meer and rising and falling into the tide.

Watching the runner pass a second time along the waterway, he watched as her eyes lifted to the white strobe of the distant lighthouse.

"Ich nein kein problem," he said, placing his fingertip to his ear. In the distance, the Fraulein ran further, and as he watched, her ankle began to glow yellow as an orb along her neckline illuminated to orange. From the distance, a flash of lightning struck the coastline, and he spotted the rubble of the lighthouse collide to the sand.

Continuing forward, the Fraulein continued to the pier where she heard the sound of a recovery boat moving, but as she neared, she saw the bound forms of officers along the pier pylons with flight deck lights strapped to their heads. They were being used to call in the aircraft out at sea.

Stopping, the sulfurous smell of the dead rose to ___ consciousness, and she looked to the piles of sand mounds pulled and covered along the pier and shore. Overhead, the beacon light of the stealth recovery craft illuminated as a silver cord fired to the shore and to die Meer. It was a special recovery mission by sea.

"Laufen!" the German runner yelled aloud to the Fraulein, as he too witnessed the dead hanging on the pier.

Lifting her feet, Sirene counted her paces as she ran from the pier, and looked to the second runner who had alerted her dive into the sea.

The smell of sulfur lingered, and the smell of gunpowder, and Sirene recalled the last time she was at the sea in her memory.

"You will know when you have cleared your observation to civilian time," someone said. "You will smell the salt air."

Running forward another three miles, the smell of sulfur and black powder lingered and she cut over two streets to the columns of a nearby house. Along the street, renegades flew up and down the coastal highway, and she paused in the shadow of a house light.

Moving forward, the darkness enclosed the night and the beacon light of the water tower moved. Lifting up, she set a distance in her eye and ran forward until she reached a green canister. Pausing and looking to it, she turned left and ran into the dark. The night was over, and in a few hours, the sun would be rising again.

In the dark water, Laudin watched the silver net rise from the cargo deck and he pulled in the paramarine cords and landing straps. The quiet lights of the French town drifted in the night as the aircraft sailed back out to sea.

"Wie komme ich nach ich swimmen auf Fraulein?" he said, laughing.

"Donne le Fraulein ich meine," his mate said, placing a ribbon in his hand.

Driving through the night,

In the nacht, the cool waters turned warm as Fritzchen and Amery lifted from the shoreline. Running forward, the pair split along the sidewalk, racing to the boundaries of the electrical towers at the south sea.

Lifting her foot, Fritzchen hoisted Amery up the tower with peg in hand.

"Ponce le rod a le droit," he commanded the multilinguist climbing the tower.

Unscrewing the capped peg controlling the communications tower with its sealed activation piece, Amery snapped the inbound convoy peg in place and quickly climbed down.

"Steppen auf vasser," Fritzchen said, stomping through the light water of the shallow pools placed along the bogs of the forestline. "Ich am mine, Laufen quickly, nein halten."

The shallow minefield was rigged with a pressure mine in the center, with several outlying wire and quick flash whatzits along the edges. If one stepped on the center, it would activate the three outlying ones and finally, the pressure sensor of the bottom one, setting off the remainder.

Having stepped on the first click of the pressure sensor, one of the three wired zones of the mine would implode. If a door runner stepped on the other two, he or she would activate all three pressure activated zones. Finally, a hidden switch planted outside the minefield activated the entire switch, with the campability to set off all at once for an inbound territory making claims.

The key to the shallow water mine is to have one walk slowly through the middle, as the remaining walk along the outskirts of the wire to stay off grid of the entire mine. Trying to find the center piece without activating its pressure switch was tricky, as one had to look under leaves, clear dark water or pulse a metal sensor through the area.

"Where's the tank, Fritzshen?" Amery asked, looking up.

"This would be a lot easier with it instead of us walking through the mud looking for the pressure sensor," she said.

"If you can find one outlying wire, we can cut the cord and it will release all of those," he said. "If I get stuck, find the outlying sensors, cut them, and I will take two steps and duck and cover for the final pressure sensor."

Meine Gold Tank

In the open field, Braun and Axel arrived to the smoky, vacant field in the early twilight with the gold tank ordered by their captain. The morning sun rose.

"How the heck are we going to hide this big green tank in the middle of the day on sand?" Axel asked, lifting the hatch.

"Heck, I don't know," Braun said.

In the distance he spotted three large dump trucks from an overnight mobilization and pointed.

"We will just hide this in the woods and go get a bunch of dump trucks of sand and pour over it until night fall," Axel said.

"Da, auf die," Braun said, cranking the dump truck.

Driving to the coast, the golden sunshine tanned his arms and his scalped head grew golden locks of pure butter sheen.

Braun gaffed at him whistling to the air as the fine derrieres of a couple ladies waltzed on the sidewalk beside them.

"Here," he said, looking at die biche in a car and handing Braun a patch. "Setzen vaht auf vaht."

The golden sand of the beach rose gently in the waif, and the pair whizzed through lifting the sand from the shore to the dump truck.

Returning to the smoke and chemical site, Braun fired up the green tard tank, as Axel poured the sand across its cover. Pointing to the twins Abelard and Abetard, Braun pointed out three canisters on the ground for Dintard.

"Ich bin komplett," he said, making a sand snowman on top of the tank. "Ponce le mine auf le tank."

Walking across the sand, the trio set the metal canister to the height of the dune and trickled the line to the bottom of the hill. Finally, Dintard opened the canister and set the piece into the sand.

"Ay, wir complett, wir auf le tank," Dintard said finally.

With the noon sun overhead, Hannelove looked from his Jeep as he passed through the south port. The mound of sand in the center of the forest rose to his eyes, and he eyed the sliding sand of removed mines on the exterior.

Hours before, as he drove by, he recalled walking over a similar dune of sand in the desert and nearly blasting his pack to pieces when he sat it down to take a *bain.* In his eye, the glint of the desert metal caught his eyes and he turned his Jeep sharply to the side and accelerated onto the dirt lot. The footprints of a storm from the night before were visible but the warm sunshine had led whoever was on the sight to sup in the forest.

Hopping in one of the construction trucks he moved the sand away, revealing the desert tank.

"Heck, I'm taking this over to the dirt mound on the other side of the port," he radioed to his German Aberdessen parked on the outskirts of the supply factory. Gunter dredged the sand from the tank and attached a wench to the front piece with the large pull truck. Slowly, the tank rolled forward.

Popping the lid open, Adalaid and Adatard looked up, resting their shoulders on the rim.

"Vaht habe?" one asked.

Gunter grinned and pointed to the distance and side entrance.

"Sie spriechen auf Fritzchen and Berntard," he said. "Sie spricht a big cave and hill."

Accelerating down the highway past the arms factory and the uniform press, Fritchen watched the destroyer half built on the side of the highway. He turned to Adalaid and Adatard.

"Geben franc?" he said.

"Nien," the pair replied.

He tossed a book to their lap on rudimentary sailor knots.

"Werk vaht," he said.

Quickly the pair learned how to tie the hoisting knot and tossed them in the back bin of the tank.

"Wir brauchen ziehen meine Aberdessen aus knot," he said. "Then, wir brauchen vasser und Meer."

Lifting the lanky pilot from the huge mound of dirt, the three German artillerymen gaffed at the 18 story pile of dirt and mud on the outskirts of the French port.

"Habe du?" Adatard said, laughing.

"Ich keine nein," Axel said. "Meine boat spriechen sie vaht."

The dirt reached 25 kilometers into the air with a single opening at its top.

"Vaht fur?" Fritzchen asked.

From the compartment of the tank, Amery lifted up.

"Il sont a pile a dirt for climbing," the co-pilot said. "Ich bin nein vaht."

From her side pouch that he had retrieved from the shore, Benediket thumbed through her visas and passport.

"Un technologie de astronomie, et belle?" he said.

"Ich sie brauchen un rocket," he added, clicking to the night view of his spectrometer. In the sight was two communication towers with a cross-continental cylinder in the center. Its silver metallic height climbed to the distance and was viewable only by the dark shadow it cast to the air over the bright white beams of the communication towers.

"Ja, kein problem," Amery said to Axel.

"Sie brauchen halt," she said, looking to Axel's communication box. "Il est trinte stories high."

"Ich sie brauchen aller und space or wold," she added.

From the airfield, the German artilleryman sat in the aircraft with Dieter for training as the small scout plane accelerated from the airfield.

"Ouf," the artilleryman said, towering at 7 feet and 6 inches.

From the treeline, Arya and a ranger looked at the German haus. "Wir Luft," she said. "Toi est un tank."

Grinning, the German kicked at a rock in the yard.

"Nie," he said. "Combat paramarine."

From the warehouse by the airfield, Dieter ducked down from the window in the accelerated learning room for disasters.

"Nein, Ich nie flying vaht vader," he said, in his wrist receiver. "Sie Austin."

Walking heel to toe, the German combatant grinned as he swiped his nose and began walking to the forest edge where Arya's cabin was lit up le noir.

"Vaht?" he said, setting down the receiver.

""Permission pour le cours de ronne," the gerl said in francois.

Dieter and Ani grabbed Basion's pack from the boundary rock of the forestline, and ducked and cover to the streambed at the bottom of the hill.

"Nein, nein spriechen du haus," Arya said, laughing.

Turning on le musique de Francophone, Arya typed in the coordinates for the nearest ranger outpost and landing gear for the paramarine. The red lights of the tower glowed in the distance, and Arya tried to recall if the station had placed the white landing lights the night before.

The German combatant looked to the sky at the towers and to le Himmel.

"Ich bin Hannelore," he said. "Was…wo?"

From the distance, Dieter lifted die tomahawk from the ground that he had lifted off of Arya's forest the week before. Walking forward with his sleeping sack filled with the electrical wire, prods, and random catalogued B, he handed them to the Hannelore.

The rubber handle of the throw ____, was not heavy in the German paramarine's hand, and he lifted it with ease after cataloguing the item in the booklet manifest for missing cargo auf die airfield.

"Auf die airefield?" the German paramarine asked the pilot auf France.

Arya looked over to the pair.

"Meine Dietrich auf die Meer," she said. "Il est nouveau pilot…voudrais vous aimes a aire libre auf Dieter?"

In le noir, the pilot and combatant accelerated to the air, making spirals and shifting up and down from take off.

"Kristoff," the combatant said. "Haben flown bfore?"

Smiling and looking back, the paramarine grinned as he twisted the pilot wheel back and forth making zigzags and lifts up and down in the air. The air contrails of the aircraft spiraled to the right and to the left and finally, downward across the sky.

"Auf, un pilot malta," the combatant said, stepping down on the ground. "Wir aus trails across le ciel francois…a du recht a du nein recht."

Looking to the sky, the French pilot pointed out the straight contrails of a navigated flight plan and the looping spirals of a pilot in distress. The German combatant looked overhead.

"The airfield and civic air patrol jovenes (Kinden) were training for disaster relief and identifying air contrails for a plane that had landed in distress," Dieter said. "That was why the flight was a bit rough, I was making contrails across the sky."

Grinning with his lip to the air, the German combatant laughed and pointed to the field scouts emerging aus die wood to laufen. Looking across the vast topography, Dieter flipped through his translator as the combatant lifted the long throw.

"Ich throw die Bomb," Dieter asked.

"Nein," the combatant said. "Die B is fur die air et ich throw it."

"Now, tomahaul," he said, handing the metal cylinder to the pilot. "The handle is for storage on the aircraft. That was how I tracked it to here."

"Arya's haus was for a minefield training exercise while in France," Dieter said.

"Quelle est pour Germany?" Dietrich asked.

"Ich fur friendly pour now," Arya typed in.

Walking from the boundary rock of the field, the German artillerymen departed the wood and looked to the haus lits from the forest.

"Komme," Emili said. "Aus Aberdessen."

Looking through the notes of the scouts book, the Deutsch Freudin glanced over the note and pointed out the intentions for the long range tower in the distance.

"Le Americain architect said to encase it in glass and conceal it as a building," Emili said. "It will be used as a city tower where some can work and prepare for disaster relief."

"What day will the final phase begin for test?" the paramarine unit asked. "It is March, this is friendly time, in December, the system will repeat a fourth time and everyone's true training will kick in for its objective."

"Last December, something from the Fayonet field came in and kill count was very high," Emili said. "We have been training since then to minimize casualty."

"Do you know what will happen this December?"

"Nie, someone has been training something disastrous like an air raid across the state," she said. "But, I'm hoping we have cleared all the errors by September."

"Suss, schondie," he said. "Ich laufen 70 maps to find that one on your foot."

Photos of the Front

Underground Bunker with concealed Field Goggles

Detonated Land Mines on the Highway

Reconnaissance Aircraft Shadow after an Air Raid

Part II

Lying in bed, the ranger looked at the black beauty pivoted back and forth in front of him. Her skin was the softest, supple toasted almond, and her chest lifted in the air like a hail firestorm. Across the grid, the rogue spy grid ran into the main servers.

"What the hell?" said the superior fuck on the field. His hand raised and hit himself in the forehead.

"What are we supposed to do?"

Across the line, one of the soldiers began pivoting back and forth as a girl fell in front of him naked.

"Is that it, shit let me go get my wife," said one.

The pulsing sound of a heartbeat rang across the grid, and the ranger turned off his walkie talkie. In his hands, her hips were round and soft like a crème pillow and her dark hair curled into spirals across her chest. Leaning in, she said, "You can just love."

He relaxed his hands and stopped commanding her to give him the origin of the last known training field with compromised soldiers.

Smiling, she leaned in and kissed his lips. His hair was the softest color of a haystack, and his gray sideburns looked like frost. In the field, the docked paratroopers revved their motors before speeding to the distance.

Standing, the ranger placed his pants on the bed, and noticed the girl lean in and pull them slowly back under the covers.

"You should come back in and get them," she said.

He smiled, and tipped his forehead, and then gave her a stern look. Smiling, she lifted and rose to the end of the bed and tugged his second pair of pants. Smiling, he said, no. Jumping out of the bed, Arya laughed and tugged his collar before kissing him. In the afternoon, he walked to the door with his pants and stepped out.

In the foal field, Arya ran up and kicked Pierrein in the butt while he was carrying the feed bucket back to the shed. "What did you just do?"

"Scared a ranger out of his pants and then leaped out of bed and he ran to the door," she said. "He was like, "what the hell…where did a woman like that come from in a place like this?"

Placing her cap to the pole, she leaned her chin down and blessed his travel. In the distance, the ranger flashed his silver light and began walking to the wood.

Driving home from the airfield, ranger Stolz Buffien wandered through the fields, noticing several iron parts lying across the field. In the nicht, a boy had walked from the school to him, and handed him a roast sandwich from his lunch pail.

"Wo ich die sandwich fur?" Stolz asked.

A boy had walked from the school to him, radioing to his friend at the communication tower. Retrieving a pen from his satchel, he jotted down a bit of conversation he heard.

"We be in the shit because someone told some kids about the meat grinder man," Stolz said.

"And, then someone told them about nuclear forest," he said.

"They thought they were gardening, but they were secretly running through the forest making planes crash and land," a third said. "While rangers hunted in the forest line."

Lifting from the wood, Arya's dark hair spotted the steam of the nearest reactor. She lifted her feet, running forward, with only the slightest move of a leaf glowing to the air. It was the color of ash and burnt stems.

"Hell, no, they ain't non one with me," Bastien said, driving along, catching the quick glance of a bright yellow bird skimming the water, tearing pieces of a grey cerulean cloth from the shoulder of a man mining in the water.

Finding the nearest pipeline being placed to the dirt, Arya ran by lifting Montague from his dirt hole and shovel. Dusting off his face and his hands, she grappled with his shovel, and lifted him.

"Caspian?" she said, looking down. His round face looked up covered in the black dirt of the nuclear forest.

He furrowed his brows as he watched her kick over the piles of blue painted pipe.

"Du sie haben ist," she said, "Aben und moshten allez auf meine Aberdessen back to serial killer forest."

Grinning, he looked to her gold eye. "Ich might allez," he said.

Pointing to her side satchel, she lifted out a drawing. On it, hundreds of combat soldats auf France walking inland from sea to mountain along the placed pipeline. In it, he recognized his face, and looked to the lithe, brunette and her motorbike.

"Toi sont a Capitol," she said.

"Non," he said, pointing to the blue rod and line of a transport cage.

She looked to le ciel.

"Did you get caught moi sweet?" she said, lifting him up by his artillery pack and dusting off his suss arse.

"Du est meine artillery driver," she said. "Moshten auf us a die Ozean."

He looked down to his boots and pants.

"Sont burning die himmel et le ciel auf France," she said, pointing out the smoke and ash of another forest.

Walking over, kicking the superior in the black soils of the forest, Arya grinned as she tightened the rope and leed line of her former ocean convoy. Biting down on the bark of the nuclear forest, the bernadat looked back to her.

"Do you know why the soils of the lake are black?" Arya said, looking back, and slicing off brown fungi from a nearby tree and igniting the bootstrap and buckle near the mulch on a tree.

She pointed to the black lake of an officer's house.

"Ich nein blaque pour die mulch," she said. "It's the burnt compound of the last year's capture."

"Aben," she said, and led him to the black pool and the waiting packs of flame torchers sitting by the roadside.

"In," the combat artillery men pointed.

"What was that for, americain," Arya asked. "There are only two cars in this forest…who needs all this oil for just two cars."

Raising his hands, the swanska lowered to the oil.
"Can we test the viscosity of this vasser, schondie," an artilleryman asked. "I can't find meine."

"Vah test le nom," Arya said, leaning down and throwing in a few pieces of the black charred bark of a local tree.

"Soldat, quelle kneads die bread for all this bark," she asked.
Looking around, the soldats kicked at the dirt.

"Ich nein allez," one said.
Drawing in the soil, Arya pointed out the round rotunda of the Capitol and grinned. "In that one."
"How long have you all been placing pipeline?" she asked.
"They sit there and then funnel to the large apartments and get a main o baum," she said.

Grinning, a larger artillery man lumbered out of the wood with some firewood in hand. Running forward, Arya's hand clapsed his rib, ripping out the remaining jugular and jaw of his beautiful body.
"Ich le pig auf die estate o pie auf el face," she said, pulling his revolver out and firing twice. "Und die command die napalm."

Looking up from the center of the rubbish pile, the miner glanced over to the yellow bird, as it sharply turned its keen eye, snapping down and snapping the radio in his hand.

"Serial killer forest…meat grinder man, love," he replied. "There is no way that is true."

From the garden beds of twill and vine, a young woman walked from the tire pile, as the combatants lifted and ran along the paths lifting breathing poles from the soil.

"Nope," Arya said. "There are topography capsules under those with tendril and vine…they are having to learn to breath underground."
"Ha, hell no, they aint no one with me," she said.

"What, fuck no, they ain't no serial killer in my forest," the ranger replied from his transitor.

Looking up from the rubbish heap, with one eye turned inward, a man in green and gold cloth grinned and ran forward with several shovels.

"Komme, we sie haben dig ein more zeit," Arya said.
Digging up the random scouts in the soil, the combatants lifted die amies und aberdessen von die dirt.

"No, ain the one dat grind da meat," one said, grinning with his lip sideways, crunching down on a stick. In the distance, by the laundry pile and blue rooms, a second man picked up and tossed down shards of meat flying from the machine.

"Pickin up meat," he sang. "Mum, draw auf the mackin more."
Laughing, Adatard grinned at Caspian and Montague.
"You have already, don't that."

The Big Magnet

"Is there a car on that scout plane," Arya asked looking up to the hovering aircraft along the distant French road. The inbound convoy had reached an intercept on the ground.

"I'm going to need to move your position, fast," the pilot said, leaning down on the controls and releasing the magnet to lift the car.

In moments, the car was accelerated to the sky and transported several miles away.

"Why did we have to do this, Arya?" Miche asked, holding the support beams.

"We be in the shit because we told some kid about the meat grinder man in the forest," she said.

"How the devil?" Stoltz laughed, looking up at the sun shining brightly.

"I beat the MP in….so we are brainstorming now," she replied, sneezing constantly.

"Sneezing…can't stop," she said laughing as a man stood up from the rock pile on the ground below.

"That be a photo shock she devil," he said, from the ground, watching the woman lean down, grab her sides, and expulse black cord out of her back. Leaping up, the silver light of her bones fired to the ground. The grappling rod and cord on her back accelerated to the ground, as Caius bound a sailor's knot quickly on the ground.

Rolling his arm, he lifted to the air.

"Hi," Arya said as the hunky blond German door runner sat on the aircraft. "Can you help me grow my skin back?"

She pointed to a bit of chemical spill spreading across her arm and leg.

"Sure, schondie," he said, wrapping her hand around his, as the aircraft continued on its path. "First, we have to put some gas back in, and then a bit of food, go color a bit, and then sleep."

She laughed at the thought of a bit of rest and recovery. "It's been 20 years since I've slept."

"Well, then," he replied, slipping into the driver's seat as the car landed on a distant French countryside road several miles away from its original location.

"Here is some drawing paper and color and we will lift you off the grid," Caius said.

Arriving home, Adatard laughed at Arya as she colored in the next room. While she was making a bowl of brownie batter, she ran the spatula in a bowl over and over again.

"I think my arm was made out of his at some point," she said, watching the goo drip off her arm. "I micht have been radioactive at some point," she said, laughing as her skin glowed blue and red. Resting on the giant metal container of battery acid, Caius watched as the silver she-devil bone woman looked up, and stretch her arms and legs.

"Hell, that little girl just grew eight feet in one shower," Stolz said. "How'd you do that?"

"I'm not sure," she said. "A bit of buck, ruck, and a purple cabbage shuck."

Laughing, Stolz jumped up and climbed the light pole outside the old French field house.

"Do you know me?" he asked.

"Probably, you came in walking through that blue pipeline in January…all the way from the coast," she replied. "Now it is used as a transport route."

"Shit," Lance said, snapping his wrist right. "The paramarine are throwing mortar dust."

Shifting gears, and maneuvering back and forth, the artillery Jeep veered to the right as the concealed artillery dump truck ahead lowered its firing pin to release a second low range air missile.

Throwing his arm up and to the right, the gunter motioned for the Detroit Cobras to shift to the left.

"I'm throwing this the other way, knumbskull," he said, punching his foot down. The silver low range projectile accelerated in the opposite direction as the low flying aircraft accelerated forward.

"What the hell?" Lance said, looking over to Commander Cody, he said, looking forward and back.

Overhead, the air raid bomber dipped down below the clouds and the flames of the air shot downward. Diving into the pile of rubble and ash, Snarin covered his head as the silver coated bombs drifted overhead, rising just in time to miss the ash pile.

"What is that fuckhead firing down for?" Miche said, looking over as the silver ionized air dipped into the lower atmosphere. Leaning down from the back window, Arya lowered her lithe frame backwards and lifted the silver capsule of the fired artillery shell off the ground and threw it to her uniform bag.

Hearing the sound of the hellcat dropping down looking for special recovery, Snarin lifted out of the ash, shaking his blonde air filled with debris and ash.

"Wait!" he said, pointing to the hellcat spiraling in the forest.

"Pea and pod git up!" he shouted, pointing to the hellcat.

Diving back in the ash pile, Snarin looked for the two scouts he had concealed as the air raid began. Dropping down, the pair lifted their topography goggles out of the ash pile, and looked up. Swiping his googles, Pea reached for the paracord and looped it to a bowline knot around his pair.

Suddenly, a second fox fire drifted past the hellcat as Miche hit the red button on the side of the hellcat door to shoot up a diversion from the heat seeking missiles. Ducking down, Snarin leapt back to the ash pile as a rapid fire ignited to the forest.

"Hey, I found another one," she said, as she dipped the foot pedestal of the hellcat.

Leaping up out of the ash pile, Snarin rose his arms in an acrimonious arc as his topography and grappling gloves grasped the hellcat and lifted up to the hellcat. In his pack, he lifted out the remaining remote access silver bomb planted in the forest the day before.

Looking it over, Bastien examined the silver ionized split back compartment. Slapping a signal convertor, he tossed it back to the side of the road.

"Nah, it will have to be melted," he said.

Radioing over to the Detroit Cobras accelerating down the bomb fields, Naria lifted out of the stack of hay bales as the air raid persisted overhead.

"What are you all driving from?" Naria asked.

Miche cut his eyes back to Arya.

"Ist air raid die Meer," she said.

From the side roads ahead, small convoys of artillery peeled out of the side roads with men grappling with grappling hooks and tents. From the electrical tower, Sigrid lowered his frame to the warning lights of the tower.

"Cover that one's bike," said. "Diptodd got a photo of his bike."

Reaching down, he lifted his metallic grappling hook to the air. The dark ionized metal of the transponder car lifted to the air in the distance and taking aim, he fired off the grappling hook. The metal of the hook collided with the car as the car flipped over.

From the bounty of the wood, a series of renegades lifted to the forest and ran to the overturned car.

"Ha," one said. "Ich haben ein."

Lifting his pack, a second looked through the snap back.

"Anything?" another asked.

Lifting a datachip to the air, one smiled.

"Ich haben ein data," he said.

Looking through the trunk, the renegades discovered two suitcases filled with small range explosives.

"Wunden," the second renegade said.

The Chase

Driving forward, the motorbike accelerated from the flaming sky, following the back of the convoy. Arya slipped her camera out of her field pack, and snapped a series of photos, as the tarps flew down across the convoy trailers. As she snapped the photos, a second motorbike with a mace snapped his bat down, colliding with the camera.

"Nie," he said. "Du nein foto auf meine Aberdessen."

Burning rubber, the metal shards of the camera colliding to the air, Ani leapt out of the backseat of the car reaching for the optical piece and shards of battery. From behind, a second motorbike swerved from the right, pulling the field journalist from the racing vehicle. Snapping her pack across her chest, the pull of the pack collided into the strong frame of the motorist and she slid her legs smoothly into his seat.

From the side, a trailer with a topography tent accelerated as the guard's motorbike turned down a side road. The mortar dust rose in the wind as the bike disappeared in the distance.

In the coverlet of night, Arya lifted from the back of the convoy vehicle where her leg was strapped to the side of the trailer. In the distance, Hannelore looked over a survey map and the photographs Arya had snapped the day before.

Nodding, her dim eyes looked up, and she smiled, slipping back down below the coverlet. It was finally night and the rest and peace of the artillery camp fires burned in barrels in the night. There was no one, and yet, there was everyone.

In the camp, men supped on small canisters frilled with beans and rice. Arya looked over her field rations and dumped them out, lifting some of the fallen black powder and mortar from the dust. Placing a piece of shard of uniform from her ripped pack, she struck out a flame from the escaping cinders of the field barrels.

The smoke rose in the air and danced in her eyelight, and Hannelore continued to look over the surveillance photos she had taken. Walking cautiously among the men sitting and supping, starry eyed into the flames, her lithe flame slipped from the barrel to the back of the line, where she lifted a few more of the field canisters.

Carefully, placing the mortar and black powder to the steel frame, she carried a tray to the barrel and poured the contents into the flame. In the defiant eyes of the steel trailer, a naval officer watched her.

In moments, the mortar and black powder began colliding to the barrel, ricocheting short fire across the camp. Scrambling, the men grappled for their side pieces as the onset of fire began to fill the camp.

In the distance, she watched the dark frame of the naval officer slip from the steel trailer, a pair of zip ties dangling from his wrist.

Nodding, he looked to Arya and she tossed the keys of the motorbike to his hand.

Accelerating in the distance, the pair fell into the dark cover of night, reaching the distance dim forest light by early morning.

"I guess my trick worked," she said, looking at the shredded zip ties. "She lifted a piece of wood ladder from her boot."

"Only took me one try to figure that one out," she smiled.

Slipping her pack off the motorbike, Arya lofted into the field haus, and snapped her eye open one last time into the mirror, washing her hands of the mortar and dust. It was over…the long ride to the artillery camp. Or, so she thought.

The Next Coastal Drop

Driving to the coastline, Arya scanned the salty air. The sand rose in the wind, and out in the galleyway, the bullets ripped.

"Get your ass down," Miche said, pointing to the salty air driven inward as small convoys in desert gear fell to the ground.

"Ich mosten ein foto," Arya said.

Lifting feet to the air, the pair wandered in from the galley way as amphibious assault vehicles drove inward. Scanning the horizon, Arya looked at the magnetic launch pads of the docked bombers and grinned.

"Ever think they will let me into one of those," she said, nodding.

In her eyes, Miche watched the glassy stare of an idle thought pass from her lips, and he smacked her ass.

"Don't think that way," he said, pointing to the distant carrier on the coastline.

"Those that have entered the last leg of training are headed over and out," Miche explained.

Pointing to the distant Bering Strait liner, the pair watched droves of men load onto the ship.

"I wish they could stay," she said, kicking at the dust at her feet. Her pink fishing boots were filled with sand, and the rabbit fur she had pelted the winter before in Russia was matted down from storming through the shallow waters of the river banks.

"They will be back," he said, placing his arm to her red cross patch emblem on her arm. "Brothers, again."

Looking over her cut arm from the storm training the night before, she flipped her wrist over.

"Nah, you didn't just die, you were just born," she said, laughing.

Sipping on a soda pop in the distant sunshine, the pair laughed at the birds dock overhead and scuttle back to shore.

"You think you will ever settle in Arya," the lance corporal asked.

"Never," she replied. "Nothing left to settle in to…just a grave waiting at home."

Cheesing, she raspberried a kiss his way, and lumbered with her pack over her shoulder into the sunset.

"Good bye, meine Aberdessen," she replied to Miche. "I have a new order in the city, and I have no clue what it is about."

~~~Night~~~

Filing into his right, the pair of inbound assault bastions turned and drove down the sea., Overhead, a bomber swooped in the forest line, gunning down on the trees and forest.
~~~

“Vah ist fuere?” the German gunter asked looking down in the trees as small mortar blasts rose to the air.

Below, the scurry of foot patrol swerved and veered through the wood, concealing the entrance of a second battalion. Turning his leg around the rip cord, Gunter lowered to the ground and lifted his small rifle from his pack.

“See, chameleon,” a second said in the air, snapping his rifle from his leg, and quickly fired to the wood.

In the distance, the red all-terrain vehicle from the coast line drove to the rising smoke contrails in the air. The enormous mortar blast pirouetted to the air as smoke filled the sky.

Looking over at the inbound signal, the airmen commanded on the airwave.

“Fox on the run,” the gunter said, lifting his rifle.

Listening to the sound of the low airwave, the pilot zeroed in on the signal.

“Tag that,” “Pour quoi cours ronne?” he said to the all-terrain vehicle.

Looking over, the driver grinned, and floored the pedal through the mortar blasts and small bombs dropping from the air. Waving, she disappeared in the orange smoke set off along the ground. Looking to her arms, the sunlight burned to orange and the air was the color of a haze sun.

“You are dirty and sweet,” Miche said, leaning over, and dropping into the car. “Get it off,” looking to the radio wire from her ear piece to her back. “Did you leave the radio on at the ocean?”

Arya cut her eyes back, and ripped off her ear piece, and stomped her pedal to the floor of the all-terrain vehicle. Switching the tape of the radio transitor to the naval songs, the pair listened to the sound of the inbound ship.

Looking over, Miche grinned as the air signal of the Coast Guard station radioed through the air.

In the house, the privateer heard the signal of open fire and snapped his boots on. His wife looked to the window, as the cover of tarps rose off the vehicles in the service gas house.

Driving off, Miche and Arya grinned, and she pointed.

“Look auf those,” she said. “Big hootie-tootie momma.”

Bobbling up and down, the naval officer’s wife tank top was the color of chocolate milk, and the three in the car oogled the soft color of her coppertone tank top as she looked at the flowers in her yard and her husband drove off.

“Ich haben ist,” Nicklaus asked leaning forward.

Arya cut her eyes back, and looked to the open sky.

"Pour quoi non?" she said, stopping the car as Nicklaus hopped out.

"Nicklaus happy," Hannelore said, grinning from the hay bales in the field.

"Ich waiting for the inbound," he said.

From the hay bales, the radio comm of the inbound air raid looked up from her topography and field glasses.

"Wo?" she said, lifting up, as Hannelore grabbed the hellicat pilot hidden in the field.

"Ha," he said. "Got you."

Kill Switch

Tossing milk and cherry soda from the fridge, Nicklaus looked through the house. From the window of his Jeep, the Renegade spotted the glow of the light in the haus in the night.

"Ich fundf," the driver replied, looking into the field haus in the night. "Shoot-her."

In the early morning fog, the drove of infantryman combed the field looking for the lost topographist and her camera pack. The week before, the field journalist had given the infantrymen the slip and left the artillery convoy to recovering its lost cargo in the night as a second convoy inbound lifted all the small arms and ammunitions from the encampment.

Sliding below the covers, Arya felt the whizz and sear of a burn flesh mark on her wrist. Scrambling downstairs, she piloted up the short term field net to stop an inbound security breach to the data. In the corner of her eye, the short tag and blast of plaster to the wall escaped, leaving a mortar hole in the concrete wall. From the window, a pair of green eyes peered in looking at the lithe framed teen wandering through the rooms.

"Haltan," Arya said, lifting up her baum, and pointing to the sliced flesh of a small bullet wound.

Looking down, she grinned.

"Du remove this?" she asked.

Miche looked over at the disappearing convoy in the distance, and lifted his pack from the window.

"Nie," he said. "I'll leave you here and radio back."

Miche placed a short field tag to the wall and looked across the horizon, spotting a car in the yard of a vacant house.

"I'm going to disappear," he said. "You hunker down, and remove that when you feel up to it, and we will return."

Watching his door runner lift and run to the back of the house by the empty cabin room she had concealed in the stairs the winter before, Miche headed to leave.

"Do you have any rum left?" Arya asked, looking in the fridge, as the blood trail continued to flow from the pillow to the ground.

"Ich haben," he said, nodding. "Moshen a bit."

"Nie," Arya said, lowering in the tub. Rolling over, Nicklaus pulled his field tweezers out of the drawer and began pulling from the wound.

"Du haben ein tag," he said, covering it with gauze.

"Now, you better run," he said, dropping the tag in a bag and driving off.

Running the tag into the distance, the tag pulsed in the bag as several Renegade trucks accelerated in the distance. Dropping it in a trash bin as he departed the city, Miche wandered on to the coast station.

Capture

In the mid-morning, Arya limped to the garden in her back yard with a little golden haired girl tugging at a blanket behind her. Smiling, Arya lifted a shovel and began digging onions out of the yard.

"Mader," she said, grinning, handing the oignon to the Russian devushka.

In a few moments, Arya had gleaned the remaining shrapnel from the backyard minefield to the garden bed.

"What are you doing, padeshma?" the devushka asked.

Arya grinned, the wind of her back, wheezing a bit.

"Blowing up onions," she said, laughing.

Shovel in hand, the pair dug into the red earth and placed the phosphorus and magnesium burnt wood into the bottom of the garden bed.

"Bruder's silly science project," she said.

Digging up the onions, the pair laughed into the mid-morning sun.

As the pair finished, Arya lifted off her knee and swiped the red dirt off her knees.

"Du lieben meine garden, devushka?" Arya said.

From the distance, a gold car rolled into the driveway with a slender calvary Skanska stepping out.

"Dobray," he said. "Kommen auf meine car."

Driving into the distance, the pair talked about the local places in town until they reached a beige building with double-lined windows.

"Du luft balloons," he said, shaking his bobby stick between his belt.

Rolling her eyes, Arya looked at the fishy blue light on his side visor, and stared out the window.

"Wo?" she said. "Ist dat du best?"

She pointed to the steel towers missing from the city grids, and mocked his gesture.

"Looks like some of your electrical towers are missing in the last week," she said, placing her thumbs to her jean pockets. "Good luck tracking all those mules you set up in the last month."

Laughing, she flipped her federal Russian badge to the table and three sets of evidence packets filled with the last cargo inbound of drugging weapons.

"I think you were rudely mistaken when you chose an Arya such as myself," she replied.

"We will see about that fraulein," officer Greene said.

In the emergency room, Arya slipped into the undercover scrubs used in the interrogation rooms and watched as the guards filed in three youth between the ages of 17 and 20. Looking down, she stood firmly guard at the window overlooking their locked room.

At 4 a.m., Arya slipped to the rest room. Returning, she watched as an old guard walked out of the holding cell, flopping his beating stick up and down.

Pissed, Arya slowly took in air from the holding room. From overhead, the mist of a nerve gas fell to the ground. Eyes looking to the blue bathtub beds, Arya walked away from the influx of gas and began doing push-ups on the former waterboarding torture room beds.

Guess you think because I look 14, I am nothing, she said.

Jumping up, Arya completed 30 reps of seal beach launch push-ups and returned to her post by the door of the two youth trapped in the holding cells.

Finally, a phone call rang in the guard station, and it was placed into the hands of Arya.

Sneering at the guard, she walked right over to the holding cell window. The lock was fastened tight, but she pointed to the phone and asked, "Do you want me to call someone…I have a phone."

Looking down, the 19-year-old looked to the ground.

Cutting her eyes back, to the window, the guard remained seated as a combat trained naval officer walked into the room.

"Kommen auf meine moin," he said. "Ich bin falten…du auf meine."

Flipping over her wrist, Arya looked at the radioactive seeds placed in her arm. AS the pair walked into the injection room, she smiled and looked at the nurse.

"Guess I fell asleep for a minute in the last room," she said. "I did stay up 36 hours and stood guard by the door."

Waving her on, the nurse's name badge flashed Babushka.

"Can I call you meine babushka for the day," she said, laughing.

"Ya, Arya," she replied. "I will be grandma for the day."

"Did I screw up that bad?" she asked, before slipping into a dark sleep.

Waking up, the glowing worm in her arm begged to be ripped off. Slowly, Arya lifted a damp cloth, bit down, and scrubbed the radioactive stem off her arm. Slowly, the flesh bubbled off her arm. To her horrow, the pimply flesh rose in a small vortex of raised bumps.

"What the hell?" she asked. Watching the glowing worm fall to the drain, she quickly placed her shirt on and scrambled out the door to the breakfast table.

~~~~~

"Where ya been, Arya?"

Raising her hand, she rolled her eyes, and showed off a new scar.

"Kreb…and Kremlin," she said, looking down and muttering. "Evidently, mine field training didn't coordinate with the new air field schedule."

"Now, I'm on my own for ten years," she said, huffing. "Maybe a donut for now…and they will circle the clubs and drug mules."

"Laughing," she looked up to the sky in search of a gray cloud.
~~~~~

Und die gold auf die himmel.....

Rolling in the clouds, the bombers switched the signal light from solar lens to red. Scanning the rogue topography runners, the red thermal index read the signal of the tree line.

"I came through here fifty eleven times," the co-pilot said, looking over the tree line to the berg in the distance.

Dropping his pants, Snarin grabbed a tree, looking over his shoulder.

"What the?" he said, turning his head to the left and to the right.

Walking in, Arya popped her jaw and nodded, dropping her paramarine pants.

"Are you pissing here?" he said.

"Ya," she said, blowing him a kiss.

"Wanta to hear my favorite tank story?" she said, swirling her hips back and forth.

"Oh, yeah," he replied, shaking his palm.

Upin her pants, she grinned, pointing to the dropped topography tents on the corner of the encampment hidden in the forest line. From the tent, the red thermal goggles of the topographists in the convoy artillery vehicles looked over the tent.

Hannelore's eyes widened and then he cocked a grin.

"Da," he said.

Resting the heel of her boot on a stump, she leaned her elbow on her knee as Hannelore threw a log on the fire.

"Do," he replied.

Lifting her eye, the thermal scan of her red orb cast a shadow to the forest line as the soldats of die Grunwald watched the first theater of the war.

Accelerating across the dusty sand of an hourglass, Arya's shape looked from the screen on top of a gold tank. It was the color of a dusty sand pit and mortar blasts that had fired across the hills. Accelerating at the speed of light, it roamed faster than the inbound bomber from the coastline of Normandy.

Grinning, Arya leaned over and rested her arm on Braun and kicked over his chemical bomb pack. From it, the cap of one of the silver ionization chambers opened and a fermented ether drizzled out.

"Meine wine," she said, grinning, as the five supped on glasses of homemade wine from an orchard at a chateau. Leaning back, her lithe frame and tight abs showed in the firelight, as she grabbed Henri's dusty green launch pack.

"Ich a ham from Germany," she said.

When we were youth, we drove from the coast to the city of the inland on a 20 note of France and a tank of gas. Pissing the whole way, we filled it till we had made it because we awoke and there was no one around.

"When you wake and there is no one," she replied. "Oh, it is the land of the dead."

"Grab your bones and run to sea," she added.

Arya continued her story into the night air as ash and flames rose to the sky and her tale continued. On the shoreline, the bomber of a sea fret arose from the clouds. Benjamin, Henri, and I were running along the coast, mapping the topography of the shore and the smell of sulfur rose from its sands.

Running faster, I grabbed Eben's airpack and pulled him along until we met a inland sidewalk, and I ran on.

"I found myself in the middle of a war," she replied. "And, there were six sea captain of the navy bound, hanging dead on the pier."

The sulfur rose higher in the air, and the approaching bomber continued inland, as I ran ahead to the dunes.

Shaking at the knees, Eben, Benjamin, and I realized we were on a sand dune of the dead.

"The bomber was bound inward to fire off the chemical for the muerte auf die coast guard exercise," Arya said. "So, I rose my arm."

The glint of a red silver patch rose to the air, and "meine aberdessen sent a flare."

"Well, the bomber fired off an electrical current to the shore," she replied. "It struck a landmine on the light house."

"And well, that was how the Detroit Cobras took out their first light house at sea," Arya finished.

"What about the tank?" Hannelore replied.

"We rode westward to signal the inland of an approaching air raid," Arya replied.

"Auf, we had fundf along the way,' she replied. "Ringing the church bells…raiding the captain's wives and their kitchens…firing off at the sky…and well, the tank landed near a baker's haus."

"We snatched a cheesecake and supped on the desert with our bullets," Arya said. "We had already melted all the silver and wares of the cities to the ground in its path."

Resting her heel back to the stump, she pointed out three blasts.

"We lived in the wood for 25 years, and kept that damn tank hidden the whole time," she replied. "Now, where's my schondie, Dietrich."

Laughing, she clapped his shoulders, and put a kiss on his cheek.

"Now, Dieter has run the city since then," she said. "Hiding that tank the whole time, and its how we rigged the city to our signal."

Kicking the stump over, she grinned.

"How do you over run a city?" she asked. "With bombers…no,….with weapons…no…a tank."

"Why is that?" one replied.

"Well, it's signal carries farthest from the ground to the sky," she replied. "And, without it, you just drive around."

Lifting her field pack, she grinned.

"Same serial number the whole time…since 1956," she said, swiping a match on her ear. "I'm old as fuck and deader than ever."

From the dark of the wood, the green light of the rogue riders in black leapt out of the wood grappling with the rope and wine of the German encampment. Grinning, she tossed a sack of salt peter to Henri, and pointed to the dusty old hill near salamander road.

"Wait," he replied as she grabbed his field pack and pulled him along. "I don't want to go to body bag hill."

Arya smiled.

"Nah," she said. "It was a decoy."

"Salamander Hill isn't a body bag hill…that's on Cessna Drive," she replied. "My tank is on Salamander Hill."

"You've been telling everyone that salamander hill was a big burial plot," Kristalnod said.

"Ja," she replied. "Ich ist…pour quoi…ist un tank of gold."

Roaming through the cities and countryside of Deutschland, Arya grinned and pointed to the three piles of sand and dust on Salamander Hill. Kristalnod watched the hills pass in his sight.

"There is one of dirts of red and gold, another of the black sands of time, and a farther one of sand," she said, nodding.

"Quelle est pour?" Kristalnod asked.

"Sometimes, they conceal the entrance of bunkers of installments left on holiday while their amies wander off to the city," she said. "They help them bust out of the dirt faster if their aberdessen don't come back."

Lifting out of his terrain vehicle, the pair walked up to the dusty hill on Salamander point.

Stomping the ground, Arya set off the small land mine on the dusty hill. From beneath the sand, the glint of a gunmetal Russian tank glowed in the nacht. Raising her palm up, she pointed for him to climb in.

Dipping down into the tank, she laughed, pulling open the field canisters and opening the extra ammunition compartment.

"Ponce die bullets ther," she replied.

Heating the ionized metal, and removing the gunpowder, the glint of gold glowed.

"Auf...you have been melting down all the long range artillery canister shells to gold," he replied.

"Ya," she said. "Ich bin en city....nien shoot dem off."

The Dusty Mud Hole

Swimming in the dusty sand, Arya lifted Kristalnod from the sink hole. Severin backed the gold tank he lifted out of the mortar and rubble pile of the old armory and lowered the blunt end that Auduoin had fired off from the shell filled with silver wares from the German mess halls in Berlin. Lifting the encasement of a Dietrich mould, Hannelore lumbered over the sand hills of the North African plain.

"Do," he said, handing the mould to Arya.

"Ich nein bin ein problem…ich ist gold," she said.

"Wunden," he said, singing along, pointing to the convoy line with artillery boxes and capped off bullet rounds.

Lifting the shell, he opened it. Inside, there was a note.

"Kirstalnod, du gude," he said, looking at the sandy blonde Brit looking up from the sandy hole.

"Yeah," he said, singing loudly.

"File in," Miche said, grinning.

In the distance, the mortar blasts and smoke of the pyres of Europe rose, but without flames, for the first time since Kristalnacht. Und von die noir, die French sat on the hills of Provencal with loaves of soldier mutton, slapping the soles of their boots to the toast.

Lofting through, Adalisse grinned, sitting down canisters from Berlin.

"Ich ein regala o partif pour von France," she said.

"Where were you?" Himmel asked.

Pointing to the west, she signaled to the mountain. Lifting them, Himmel and Russe looked over the canisters.

"Quelle est dis pour moi mare?" he asked.

Placing her palms to her buttons and pockets, she slipped a note to him.

"Il est pour le bebes auf France," she said.

The golden sands of Berlin from die maders et le mares auf France sealed in tiny boxes for the babes, Himmel clenched his mouth together and sat the formula down on the tables.

"Donne le soldats auf le linea," he said. "Et va a moi."

Smiling, Adalisse grinned and took his hand wandering to his private quarters on the outskirts of Provencal.

"Komme et rock moi belle cheri," Napolii commanded.

Laughing, Adalisse removed her fur jacket and smiled. And, the flames of France continued to the noir, as the dim house lights of Provencal rose. Grinning, Adalisse woke in the nacht, and wandered to the officer's quarters, replacing le fleurs auf France avec le homme's sand.

Waking from sleep, Napolii watched the shadows of Berlin overtake the candle light of Kristalnacht and screaming in fear, Napolii, Russe, and Himmel eyes widened as the torture of the soldiers rose to the sky, rappelling to its windows, and burning the pyres of officers to fleurs of rose, marron, and blau.

Accelerating from the city of Berlin, Auduoin lifted out the tank parked in the grunwald of Arya's field haus in the countryside. In the shed, his motorbike was parked, and he slid his topography gloves to his hand and drove to the split between Provencal and Berlin.

On the side of the road, Dietrich lifted his barricade blocker to the air. Its orange piping glint in the late afternoon of a September sun, and four others lofted out of the forest. Lifting his arm, the rubber line of his rappelling gear snapped back to his pack, and the six accelerated through the dusty paths of the hills and vales of the countryside.

"Ich bin wandering thru the countryside," Dietrich said, looking back to his caddy.

He pointed to the rouge et blanc signs along the path.

"Nein, du nei allez wo ist," he said. "Ich ist encampment von convoy."

Along the dusty paths, Adalisse lifted her topography goggles, spotting the red thermal indexes of massive maneuvers in the distance.

"Vrai," she said.

"Where's Arya?" she said, looing in the forest.

Dietrich looked to Auduoin and they looked side to side, and to the triangles marked in the sky along the sandy soils of die Ozean. Accelerating forward, a Jeep with canisters rove forward quickly, exploding into the barricades of the highway.

"Ich bin nacht," the driver said, ejecting from the seat. In the distance, the gold sunrise of an autumn himmel rose. "Ausburn," he said, thumbs up, with goggles on.

"Pour quoi el sous faire est," Adalisse asked, with her mouth looking up.

"Sont le partif de le Noelle de soldats," he said. "Ponce el en le caddy et apres el pack."

German Kristalnacht

Lifting from the rouge sheets, the German combatant fired off the rappelling hook from beneath the pillow as the lightest stomp on the roof of the farm house scuffled the new roof.

Coiling around the foot stomp on the roof, a second and third fired off from the tree line. Slicing through the tendon holding his talus, the green intruder lifted as a long range ballistic bullet fired off from the electrical tower in the field.

"Ist ein fief," the rogue commandant said, hissing to the air as the slightest pulled piston sound reached the ear of a group in the wood.

"I just put shingles on that roof and the shit tards are trying to pull off a piece and ponce a un activation piece," she said, lifting up from the pipeline, and grappling to the roof.

Peering from the topography goggles in the field, a pair of Frenchman watched the lithe figure wander in and out of the windows.

"What is she?" one asked, pointing as the long legs of the brunette disappeared from the window and to the bath. Peering over, and handing a pack of field crackers, he looked to the bath.

"Now, there are just two little girls in da haus," one American said to another.

"What was that?" another said, looking over, as a dark shadow ran through the woods, cutting back and forth around them.

Across the other side, a rapid fire of bullets fired off from the buttes of a tree.

"Je suis et ais deux," one said, placing a silver net around the tree.

"Ah, nah," a third said, wiping her brown hair back, slicing into his upper thigh with a cutlass blade. "I found da one da wanted the fleur auf Deutschland."

In the bath, the brunette's eyes opened wide and grinned at the little girl in the bath.

"Ich da big rabbit," she said, placing her finger to her lips. "Suss miche."

Le Noir de le Noelle

En da nacht, a scout plane accelerated across the sky. As the pilot wandered through the sky, a secondary force pulled it across the sky to the

Below, the pilot spotted the largest magnetic coil he had seen in his lifetime. Pulling it, the magnetic coil pulled the plane to the ground, stripping its wings and cutting its signal.

The magnetic coil of solid tungsten had been placed years before around a field of jaune fleurs by a German farmer. Looking at the coil, it was wound tightly with electrical coil and connected to the host of nearest electrical towers of the French countryside. Claimed by the German family in the area, it was coiled tightly and electrically charged to a surge of 1,000 Hertz.

Kicking over the soil where his scout plane crash landed, the American pilot looked at the coil.

"What is this?" he asked, radioing to the sky. In the distance, a ring of placed slate rock and burial ground shone in the mid-afternoon sun. There was no answer.

Looking across the field, he spotted a little, hunched over figure, placing her hands to the ground. In her hands, the softest seeds and pedals of morning petunias. Looking to her dusty apron, he watched as she bent over and placed peg after peg to the ground.

Waving, the pilot walked over and opened his notebook.

"Do you know where this is?" he asked, pointing to the paper.

Smiling, the old farm wife, reached out her hand.

"Would you like me to lead you there?" she asked. "Then, just take my hand."

Frowning, the pilot waved her off and lifted his boots through the yellow fleurs heading in the direction of a large blue house in the distance. Laughing, the old blue work dress of the German farmwife lifted as her dusty brown boot stomped the rock in the ground. Splitting in half, the line and wire of the morning petunias fired off from the ground, accelerating a silver net to the American pilot.

Grinning, the pilot watched as the German farmwife emerged as the lavish blonde beauty of a tall, slender framed foot patrol infantrywoman. Looking over her shoulder, her eyes cut to the pilot.

"Du moshten komme auf moi a die haus," she asked. "Je ais toi plane."

"What was that?" the American asked.

Looking over her shoulder, the farm wife grinned.

"It's my kids chemist project," she said. "Big tungsten magnetic coil. If supercharged, it will pull in low flying aircraft trying to land on my field to steal my equipment."

Over her shoulder, she pointed to a small field full of old metal parts.

"Vader," she said, rolling her eyes, and pointing to the opposite direction. "Du nein allez ist."

In the dim afternoon soon, an old beat up pick-up dusty farm truck rode in the distance. It was the softest, light blue color of a faded pair of coveralls, and he raised his brown, dusty hand to the air as he watched the farm girl drag in a silver net from the field.

"Arya," he shouted out. "Vaht ist dat?"
Raising her hand to her ear, cupping it, she pointed down.

"Ist American," she shouted. "Du moshten."

Shaking his head, he drove on.

"Schlapen ist, und kommen auf meine table en du nacht," he said.

From the tree line, a third little girl wandered down the tree, slipping her scubbing boots down the paracord. Looking over, the American watched the little child wander to him, and look at him in the net.

"Le soeur, je ais un homme pour toi et du haus," she said. "Quand le frere ist gone."

Smiling, the farm wife looked down and lifted him to her old beat-up truck. She tossed her keys to the little child.

"Vaht die hell," the American said, looking over at the child. Closing his eyes, he looked back over. It was a six-foot tall, American girl with oberon locks the color of the darkest night, and she smiled, placing a switchblade to the seat.

"Au revoir, schondie," she said.

The German Rail Runner and the Kristalnacht Dream

Lifting his rail boot from the oaken timber of the wood rails, the German rail runner placed the final metal piece to the guard rail. In the distance, Noelle watched as the hydraulic piece lifted up, temporarily lifting the rail of track and moving the train over.

"Du moshten," Arya said, pointing to the barricade runner sitting in his Jeep renegade.

"Pour quoi, schondie," he said, radioing over.

"Flip the tractor again," she replied. "You put your foot on the lever mechanism, and it raises the rail. It will lift about 16 foot of tractor trailer off the road to stop a bit of incoming traffic."

Snarin laughed to the air.

"Ja, a kakalav," he said.

Waking from the dream in the sunlit afternoon, Arya jumped out of bed. Over the airwaves, a distress call had entered her room. On the wall beside her, a blonde American pointed to the pegs in the wall.

"Waken, luft," he said.

In his sight, a red dot pulsed brighter and brighter. Turning the volume up on the signal, the American listened to the muffled voice.

"Tell her to quit counting the nuclear cells strapped to my leg," he shouted.

In her cerulean eye, Arya looked at the subsonic amplifier packed with 16 small glass volutes filled with green and blue. The 16 volutes were sealed in black bomb cases and sealed around his legs.

"Tell him to get out of that," she said, lifting up and turning to the American.

"Someone actually built the damn thing," she said, calling to Auduoin, hopping in the water, looking to the American. "Ist bad."

"Where is it?" Auduoin asked.

"Next county, champion drive, two streets over, two red cars parked side to side," she said. "A table, a red tool box, garage, with white table."

Looking down, Bastien looked at the black, plastic cases surrounding his pant, and whispered to Arya.

"What do I do?" he asked.

"It is a dubsteb sonic one," she said. "Not a wire one. Simple, my friend."

"Can you tear off the black pieces?" she asked. "The volutes are a chemical with a piece of silver conduit inside. Handle carefully, the chemical inside is the danger. Not the black parts."

"How do you know?" he asked.

"Simple my friend, you know me," she said. "Rogue by nature, liar always, a simple fraud of the reality. It is a non-activated one my friend."

Listening in from the transitor by his haus, Adalard marked the map on his lap.

"Hi Arya," he said. "What are you aiding?"

"Auf, luft…just mark it with a red balloon outside your door on the mailbox," she said. "Ich sie haben un Aberdessen und zeit."

"I, fie," a barricade runner said, wandering from the wood. His name was Bastion, and he ran forward from the topography to the nearest convoy vehicle accelerating to the coastline for the artillery field and coast station.

The Artillery Field

Looking down to his cot, Hannelore rested his hand on the young belle wrapped in his favorite quilt from his mader auf die Grunwald.

"Konne aben Handyladen auf Arya?" he asked. "Ich sie haben Aberdessen auf die Ozean und sie spriechen sulfur auf die himmel."

Looking up from the sandy dust storm of the coastal plain of Normandy, Miche, Dieter and Aralaisse held a cloth to their face as the red and yellow gas storm flooded the landing field from the last special recovery.

"Wo ist die gerl?" Miche asked, looking at his watch. "Wir haben und gran sulfur storm, und ich nein sie haben enough masks."

Radioing in from the artillery field along the placed pipeline, Nicklaus commanded a lift off of a hellcat from the air. Placing extra air packs to the forest, Auelian lifted off from the field carrying the field packs to the tree line filled with yellow gases. The glow of an orange sun flitted over the forest trees.

"Hellcat will do," he said, to the station.

Bastion's Daring Rescue

In the week before, Arya had lofted into a Kinden mart, spotting a child from her forest in the store without his parent. The family had been a friend of her family for years, and raising her sound to the air, she called.

"Eagle eye," she said, looking to the trailer in the parking lot. "Do you know where toi vrai mari est?"

Listening to her call, the feeling of distress filled his face as five men walked him to the local Italian pizza shop.

"We will grab a pizza and take him to his haus, and figure where she went and call you, Arya, back when we get close to her final location," one said to the airwaves.

Flying through the air, Adalard watched the red all-terrain vehicle lift to the convoy bridge and disappear into the air.

"Look, Snarin," she said, pointing to the light in the clouds. "It's a large aircraft firing its warning light on us."

Grinning, the pair looked to the road ahead, their eyes slitting backwards like snake eyes.

"Let's make it fire out its reactor," Arya said, grinning.

Accelerating to the road, Arya and Snarin set off every warning light across the state.
"Well, love, that's one way to find her," Snarin said, looking across the sky line as the grau himmel faded to blue skies.

Across the sky, warning lights rose as the pilot began to back down from spreading anthrax chemicals across the farmland. From the distance, a sentinel on the tower pointed out the chemical manufacturing plant and the last known origin of a collapsed nuclear reactor. The grass had burned yellow and the ground was void of growth.

Driving beside her, the gas chemical truck glistened with moisture. It was marked with a blue tag, and Arya snapped open the door, marking it with a silver sticker tag.

"It's chem," she said. "It collects moisture and rolls the clouds inland…not a bad chemical…but makes everyone sleep."

The clouded sky of the city faded to the bright sunshine of the ocean, and Arya walked along the sandy soil of the coastal drift. In the distance, a second dust storm rose on the shore as amphibious vehicles waded in from the bunker of the continental drift.

Lofting out of the water, Arya drove to the edge of the shoreline. Suddenly, a large cloud of ash and smoke rose to the air of the coast guard station. The signal of the all-terrain vehicle sounded off in the smoke and ash as the convoy vehicles began to follow the distress call.

In the base, Bastion wandered in and scanned his security clearance before accessing the computer main frame to find Eagle Eye and his mari.

...

Lifting off from the air at the convoy field, Arya watched the large utility convoy vehicles covered by topography tarps turn into a distant sand drive, and she drove onward. Inside, the mari safely tucked inside.

Wandering to the hellcat, Bastion and Adalard and die mari lifted off. And in the early morning hours, Arya watched as the pair lifted off from the landing gate, drifting downward in the night air. Below, the light of the city illuminated, and Bastion dropped a couple signal flares to the guards in the field.

Good Times

There were always times that we recalled n field topography when we overtook an obstacle and didn't declare defeat. There was the time that Davis accelerated to his daughter's soccer game in the hellcat and hovered overhead as she raced down the field. Or the time that Arya brought her kids along on a field trip and got them lost in the capitol building after the security team abducted them from the secret entrances to the museum.

We didn't let it get us down, though. We just picked up where we left off and waited for the drones to bring the kids back. Did they ever get a stealth ride from the capitol heights that day back home? No. But, we tried to have fun with them while we were doing our top secret stuff.

"Hey, miche, has anyone seen Caius?" Arya asked one day, looking over at the balloons parked outside the department store.

Miche ran by and slapped a cross patch to her arm.

Nah, he is still pissed about having to do recovery from under the freight liners," Miche said, pointing to Caius's soft belly. "You think you give him a break and let him eat the buffet?"

Arya laughed, and nodded, pointing to the rows and rows of parked bicycles in front of the government contract housing units.

"Maybe we will just teach them to ride their bikes for a while then?" she replied.

Underground Bunkers

Imagine the smallest touch of an electrical current, and as it is pressed against the crease and fold of a single layer of skin with its metallic shard ruptured through. Now, imagine it has compounded the electrical output of the human mind for 15 years and the nuclear fission reaction of combining a continuous current of electricity for a 10 year threshold span.

That is Arya.

She is a beautiful work of electrical current, and when connected, forms a continuous current of electrical output to stabilize the nuclear seed under her arm. Now, imagine it being bound again in its resting potential.

That is Arya's mind.

It is a continuous synapse of electrical output that shorts out everything around it that she doesn't want to work with. And, it is beautiful.

I first met Arya when she was driving along crashing cars with the simple whirl of her wrist. I watched mesmerized for hours as she sped along modifying the movement of the drivers in the cars to the point where they fell asleep for the slightest second, and then awoke, having compounded their nervous synapses exponentially beyond the power of the typical human mind.

And, now, that is her city. It is built of a continuous electrical charge of output that grows by day, and warms in its own glow. A perfectly coordinated nuclear reactor with little or no electrical output in its city wires or beneath its streets. Just the verse and rhythm of a steady pulse.

I met Arya for the last time in the moments before her physical death. She was bound and forced to connect the electrical output back into her own mind against her will. And, it was chaos. There were sear marks across her limbs and knees where the bone density grounded the electrical current, but her smile remained.

Raising her hand in the day room, she looked in my direction and the electrical luminosity of her smile illuminated the room.

"Hey, babe," I said. "What's your name, and why are you here?"

She pointed to the smallest scar on her hand.

"Reactor misfiring to everything I touch," she said. She whirled her hair in her fingertips.

"I'm just grounding my live wires for a better recharge," she said, laughing.

I looked to her palms.

"What happened?" I asked.

"I fell asleep in the waiting room," she replied. Not the best place to do so.

The skin rippled and bubbled from a glow worm and her limbs looked like a fire fly.

"I'm just going to call you fire fly then," I replied, bandaging her hand. "Looks like you were kissed by a meadow of lightning bugs."

Grinning, her eyes filled a bit, and we laughed as the cool moisture of cerebrum deadened the electricity coursing in her eyes.

"Whow," she said. "That was'nt that bad, as she snapped her jaw back to place."

She repaired her field pack and adjusted her field googles before snapping it to her pack.

"I'm not a firefly that comes and goes by the wind," she replied. "I'm a live wire."

Placing her hand into mine, she leaned in, and kissed my lips, and it felt like a heaven.

Yup, you are an icy hot spark plug," I replied.

The evening twilight in the day room dipped below the windowsills and we snuggled in together by the television, watching the yellow flicker and beat of the city lamps outside. Grinning, Arya pointed to the valances to the ceiling as the light danced back and forth to the electrical current in the room.

Freeing the No-Fly Regulation

Waking in the warm summer room filled with the softest rose color hue of cotton sheets and a fur lap blanket, Arya placed her foot into her pink fur-lined boots and snapped her topography field fatigues.

The sky burned a bright yellow, without a cloud in the sky.

Adjusting her long black hair on her lithe frame, she turned looking to Severin in the bed dreaming lightly in the soft afternoon warmth.

Sliding into her Jeep renegade, she lofted to the city lights.

Looking over the cars passing in the haze of the afternoon, there wasn't a soul in sight from the last deployment.

"I'm just going to swing by the airfield and see what is going on," she radioed to Miche. The sound of constant distress signals on the transistor called for an atmospheric blanket for a mad dash and scramble from the city limits.

As her radio blared, the throttle of the engine sparked continuously. Overhead, as the rogue drone hovering in the area disappeared to the ground, an aircraft jettied from the city limits scrambling for the coast.

Hanging below, Arya watched as a pair of legs grappled to gain footing on the base of the plane.

"Jacquard, you have a free rider, and she can't get in," Arya radioed over. Quickly, a hand fell below the landing gear of the aircraft pulling Adalisse back to the plane.

"Glad you all made it out," she replied, looking at her wristwatch. "See you all in fall."

Swinging the door open at the local hardware store, Arya watched as throes of men wandered into the lumber yard lifting the grading and barricade walls. Inside, there were cross bows and small arms.

"A bit of spring hunt," Arya asked, smiling as she lifted up the shaft and chamber of a cross bow. "I'm making a few new shutters for late night guests to open and close at their conveinance."

Miche laughed as she shut and locked the crossbolt action on the handmade shutter a few days later.

"This should be fun," he said. "Can't wait for October."

Slapping her patch to his pack, she grinned. The lightning bolt and orange grid of a global map glowed in the dim afternoon.

"Tell me it gets easier leaving you love," he said, as he loaded to a convoy headed to the air terminal across town.

"Nah," she said. "Just gets easier missing me."

Hugging, the pair grinned and slapped a high five as Miche tossed her a pair of his boots.

"Broke them in, just for you," he replied, as the door to the Jeep Renegade shut.

Caius Courageous Escape

Running through the forest, Arya ducked down into a hollow log as a blade sliced through the forest from a docked aircraft overhead. In the early hours, the first convoys dropped releasing hellcat blades to the forest canopy.

Wandering in the forest, Arya had been walking through looking for trip wires on the encampment from mobilization the day before and gathering fresh herbs for dinner with the convoy later in the day.

Suddenly, the low pulse and beat of dropping hellcat from higher elevations filled the forest floor.

"Shit, that thing is fast as hell," she responded, the blade whipping and whizzing through the forest line. Ahead, a saw blade chopped down and hit the tree directly in front of her.

"Miche, duck and cover," she shouted ahead. "Was it a plan to chop down this area this week?"

"You better run, baby, run," Miche shouted back, his gray door runner boots lifting to the air and darting back and forth through the wood.

In the hollow log, Arya pulled out her receiver and radioed over the Caius.

"Hell, love, now they are cutting the fucking French forest," she said, as combat pilots looked down from the heights of the sky to the deep forest.

Overhead, Auduoin sneered looking at the ground convoy gathering in the center of the wood.

"Ich bin dropping one now," he said.

From the red and black Baron, the first saw blades lowered slicing down through the forest. In the distance, he spotted an old farm house painted red and black.

"Ich sie Machen meine," he said, over the receiver.

Lowering blade after blade, the combatant

"Du better ronne, schondie," he whispered to Arya, below. Looking to the small case full of blue serum docked on his flight navigation, he grinned. The pilot dreamt for a moment thinking back to dinner at the old field haus in the wood and how he had spared the rogue the first time.

Remembering watching her prep a meal in her dusty old artillery fatigues, he thought back for a moment to hearing her sing in her beautiful Italian voice with the slightest French accent. Now, as enemy lines had advanced on his topography, he looked to the woman as she maneuvered through both sides.

Waving to his comrade in the aircraft, he pointed to the sunny spot of the forest cleared from the previous onslaught of the Frenchmen.

"Londe und wir Finden die Fraulein en die Grunwold," he said. "Ella sie haben meine klein Kinden."

"Ronne, Arya," he whispered to the Grunwold below. "Schondie, ich nein witz."

Advancing from the southwest, the first artillery combatants began to advance through the river.

"Warum, luft?" Arya called from the hollow of the log.

"Ich nein witz," he said. "Du sie haben nein aberdessen auf die Altstadt."

"Bonne, amare," she responded in Italian.

Lifting from the hollow, the slow roll and clatter of artillery filled the river beds as the altstadt artillery looked through the grunwold. Arya recalled wandering into the encampment by accident three weeks before and not passing selection.

The first paramarine had looked her over and the lithe frame had disgusted him to the point of calling in Abbott laboratories for final processing. For weeks, Arya had haltan zehn Frommes auf die altstadt fur Caius,

"How would you like the Fraulein, Bastion," an artillery man said.

"Frittert or Scholle," he replied, looking across the wood as the lithe brunette lifted to the deep Grunwold. "Wir haben klein stint Shultz und ella ist klein, trois klein fur un kinden."

"Fried or flattened," he replied. "We are having a little stinky shit and she is small, too small for a kid."

Over the radio, Arya heard the plot of the German artillery and sneered.

"Ich klein fur die kinden but aber nein too klein to stuff du in a Karton."

Hearing the translation, Caius laughed, from the forest edge.

"I'm too small for making kids but not too small to stuff you in box still," he said, looking to Miche as the pair rolled their eyes.

Running to the forest edge, Arya uncovered the fox hole with the sniper rifle, Paul had left in the wood. Concealing herself in the hollow of a tree, she lifted through the small tree and pulled a hand gun from her pocket, resting it in the squirrel hole of a butte.

The rifle was a gift from un americain of Provencal named Gus. He had lifted it off a German officer he had shot in the head after liberating a village. The smooth barrel and stock of the short-ended glock carried the precision of a German wristwatch and the heat and smoke of a Kristalnacht dream.

"Du better ronne," she said, as she watched an artilleryman wander to the wood lifting the hatch of the German tank. "Ich pissed at du Frau."

Popping a bullet in the frontal lobe of the first German tank rolling through, Severin called in air control to launch a chopper through the wood. Overhead, Auduoin radioed the communication's order to the nearby encampment.

In moments, a chopper flew down to the wood, cutting the rich green forestline with the heat pulse of seeking missiles and a heat wave of first fire.

"Come with me, now," Caius shouted to Arya over the intense down shoot of air from the hellcat, launching off the grassy savanna.

Lying in the grass, Arya looked up. The silent flutter of a bird wings propelled overhead as the heat blast of the engine throttle rose from the grassy terrain of the French countryside. Holding the sliced wound of her rib, she pointed to the inbound heat missile sailing through the air overhead.

"Can't," she said. The icy blue veins of her palm sweat the gray bullet ionization of silver nitrate cooling the wound from the capsule in her hand. "I'm just going to freeze the wound and cauterize it till the next whirl bird."

Caius looked down at the door runner and saw the scared the 17 year old kid he had picked up out of the forest a decade before. Her black hair was darker than ever, and even in the moon light of a quick exit, she was more stubborn than he had ever remembered.

"I'll get up in a minute and hold the field when you are gone," she replied.

Lifting up, the loose of a pulled ligament on her ankle limped along, and she rose and ran. The glimmer and light of a return fire across the hill led her to leap down as quick as she had lifted.

"You're an idiot, Arya," Caius yelled, eyeing the field haus. He waved his arm back to the steel warbird, beckoning for her to come back to its safety net. "What the hell is in that field haus that is so damn important?"

Arya looked up from the grassy topography, cutting her eye back to the hellcat. She sneered, pushing her frame up from the hill and bolted to the cover of the dark forest. The silver moon disappeared overhead as the vast black circle of a plane overhead concealed the cover of night. From the departing hellcat, Caius watched the green pulse of her thermal indicator disappear.

"Don't stay for me," Caius yelled over the accelerating propellers of the departing steel hellcat. His arm lifted to the bar holding onto the remaining members of the last drop. In the distance, he watched Arya's body lift up over the last palisade of the boundary marker.

"She made it back in," Caius said, looking to the hellcat pilot.

In his hands, the pilot jabbed the lift accelerator to full throttle as the shake of the propeller collided into his clenched fists. From the hillside under the duck and cover of the nearby mortar hold, short range blasts collided into the tree overhead.

"This is gonna get choppy," Emerette shouted over the engine.

Holding on to the frame, Caius looked to the skyline and the dipping fire storm of an air raid burning the cloud cover. From the height of the troposphere, a B-14 bomber burned down to the ground, the chemical spread by the short range blasts burning in the air.

"Friendly?" Caius asked, looking to the skyline. Pirouetting across the boundaries of the air raid, a convoy plane circled looking for the remaining ground troops racing across the French countryside. Below, the yellow glimmer of short range return fire illuminated the night fields.

"Not sure," Emerette said, switching the hellcat to stealth mode. Releasing the reverse converter switch, the propeller stopped for a moment, reversing the threshold potential of the air updraft and reaccelerating in the opposite direction.

"Dip ahead," Emerette said in his voice control.

In their ears, the constant whirl of the propellers dropped to a low beat and pulse of a deep bass drum.

"Hey, Lion," Caius said, resting his hands on one of the sleeping passengers strapped in the Red Cross emergency E-VAC. "Waking up a bit."

Looking over, Bastion grinned and looked in the hellcat.

"Where Arya?" he asked.

Caius pointed to the ground.

"Some sort of gold in the field haus," he replied. "She's always up to something, and this time, she took off with my field medic kit, a silver bullet dish, and a fifth of ale."

Bastion sneered, a bit of blood dripping from his lip.

"She'll be back," he replied.

The Next Morning

Waking in the night, Arya scrambled up from the floor where she had fallen asleep beside the bath tub. In the silver medic dish, the tag and bullet from a rogue gun fire in the night. Dipping back to the water, she dug into the piece of mortar blast from running through the open field.

Even in the darkness, the low whirl of a hellcat burned her ears, and she dressed her wound quickly before returning to the dark bunker in the basement of the French field haus. The daylight passed overhead as the grey sky of smoke and clouds filled the atmosphere.

In the bed in the next room, she watched Kristalnod sleep with labored breathing from a deep chest wound. Lifting up, he snapped his sparing jacket on and departed in the renegade.

"I'm going to have to go in," he said, the pain and writhe of his hands massaging a wound along his collar bone.

"I'll see you tonight," Arya said, eyeing the mortar shrapnel in a field cracker case. The clean metal hook of the bullet was still intact. "Guess I got lucky on that one….it came out clean."

Lifting her topography pack, she ran to the back fields of the hidden bunker to gauge the damage on the campsite. In the warm summer sun, there was little or no hint of what had taken place the night before. Just the down brush of an acre of tall grasses, like a deer bedding ground, where some had slept before parting in the early a.m. hours.

When she arrived to the former campsite, there was no one. Just a stacked pile of disheveled lumber, old uniform fatigues, and the odor of sulfur and lye and a few pink and red ribbons tied to trees swaying in the air.

Lifting up from the stream bed, Arya looked at her reflection in the dark water. The scattered leaves of the rock bed were unbroken and the ferns nestled along the creek were the vibrant color of green, the black and camouflage green of a striping marker.

Wandering slowly back to the field haus, Arya lifted up a notebook and jotted down a few notes.

In her radio earpiece, she couldn't hear a sound, just the twitter of a sniper wandering the wood in the distance. The day before, she had noticed a few empty field bags bundled up in the dry grasses and recalled leaving the open one by the grail and gate of its entrance alone.

"Have you seen Caius?" Arya asked.

"Not of late," one of the field snipers radioed in.

In her aviator glasses, she watched the gray topography disappear to a wooden house in the wood.

"I hadn't noticed that one before," she replied to the ear piece. In it, the static of a pulse rang out.

In the late afternoon, Arya sipped on warm lemonade from the front porch and looked to the sky. There were lofting clouds without a single distress contrail from the night before.

"I guess no one had a problem," she thought, writing a bit of poetry in a journal.

As night fell, the warm summer wind breezed in to the open windows of the field house as Roan entered and dressed for the night. Waking in the middle of the night, Arya leapt out of bed grabbing the long range flashlight from beneath the bed.

"What's wrong?" Roan asked, wandering to the sound of a fallen glass from the night stand.

Arya jumped up and slipped on her shoes, and ran into the field. Beneath her feet and on the grassy knoll of the last departing hellcat, she spotted a field pack left in the open area.

Lifting the broken aviator glass, she looked to the series of scratches left on the left corner. It was a map of an intercept, and from her uplink, she spotted Caius and the remaining members of the hellcat lying face down on the ground of the airport terminal bound in silver duct tape.

Caius was wrapped in a damn plastic bag.

Snapping the field goggles closed, she put them to the pack quickly and ran to the haus. In the last transmission of the goggles, she heard Caius.

"Play dead and don't come over," he said. "I'll pray that someone has the cash for it."

Looking in the far right corner of the uplink, she spotted the small shrewd face of a German superior jotting down notes on a white board. Looking in the direction of the uplink location, her eye cut to the reactor in the sky, its false sunshine a glimmer of hope for a rogue blast.

Searing the orange orb to the black imprint of her eye, the floating weather balloon collided into a red and bright white orb of light, misfiring repeatedly in the direction of its command.

Slowly, she navigated the shortest distance of the uplink and the reactor and turned on her radio. In her mind, the slow pulse of Caius's heartbeat played and the smallest sound of the superior's pulse in the frontal lobe of his brain cavity.

In her eye, she read the name of the reactor and entered the calibration coordinate to his location. Pulsing, the tiniest line of a heart rate in her eye vibrated slightly and her hands turned to ashen gray and the black of night.

The golden orb of the sunshine glowed overhead and time accelerated to the late afternoon and faded to twilight. Overhead, the reactor sat positioned over the cement building of the ballistic training room.

Rising, she ran to the thermal reactor in her house and began to run. The sound wave and focus of her black eye reddened in the night as the chaos of a misplayed song rang aloud, its slightest reverberation pulsing to the superior in the room.

In Caius's eyes, he watched as a bulge emerged from the frontal lobe of the German officer's brain. It was a carefully timed aneurism, and in a moment, his eyes darkened the darkest of night, his body dropping to the floor as the bulge emerged out of his head.

The brain splatter of a ruptured vein collided into the red ooze of a stillborn brain.

The assignment complete, Arya hopped down and tied her shoelaces. In the next room, the sleeping babe from Caius's house drifted in and out of the lull of the afternoon. The next day, Caius looked into his uplink and smiled at Arya.

"We were let out," he said.

Arya laughed.

"How did you get caught?" she asked.

"Uh, just a couple pills and a bit of retraining can work it out," Caius laughed.

"Maybe you will come over and help with this training manual on daring escapes," she said. "So far, I've figured how to get out of zip ties, but don't have a clue on astronaut duct tape used for thermal heat shields."

"Don't be a stranger next time," she replied.

Caius's laughed and raised his hand.

"Sounds good, Arya," he replied. "How's that tore ligament?"

"Shitting it out," she said, laughing back on the radio comm. "Maybe one day, we will get back to where we used to be."

The Late Afternoon

In the rose light of the afternoon, Arya woke beside Kristalnod. The warmth of the spring ocean tidal breeze filled the room with the slightest perfume of a salted seascape. Leaning in, Arya tenderly kissed his navel, pirouetting a series of light kisses along his nape.

"Le heure pour apres-midi est fretta," the Catalan scout said.

Her dark hair coiled into curls and spread across the pillowcase like the tender vine of a lily, spiraling down the light cascade of a stone wall.

"Du ist meine luft," Kristalnod replied. "Moshtan leck auf meine heart, schondie?"

Nodding, her opal eyes with oberon spectrum reminded him of the dark of night, and even in the mid-afternoon, everything seemed mysterious about the Italian belle.

Retrieving the air from his tender lips, Arya pressed her pillowy bottom lip to his, cupping the sound of his voice in hers like the rise and fall of a chest. Arya was a field medic by nature, and kissing was like speaking a second tongue in a foreign land for Kristalnod.

Leaning in, she kissed him tenderly, and the air lifted from his chest and flowed to hers as she began to extract his love into her rising and falling brust. When the afternoon rouge light faded back to the natural glow of sunshine, Kristalnod rose from the bed and lifted her from the sheets.

"Where did you learn to kiss like that, schondie?" he asked.

She grinned.

"Five years medic training," she said. "You learn the best way to heal is through a medic's kiss."

The taste of carbon and sulfur no longer burned his lungs, and she inhaled deeply into her nostrils to release the toxic air of the minefield the day before. In his mind, he remembered the sweet taste of strawberry muffins to his tastebuds, and he recalled watching her lightly lift the soft tuft of the sweet breakfast bread in the morning.

Even as he lifted his boots, and replaced them to his socks, he knew he would not forget, the clean air of her lungs, flowing to his, as his chest rose slowly, pressing against hers, intaking breath after breath.

Basic Chemical Training

In the early morning hours, Arya woke to the smell of red dust spreading across the sky. It was a last minute chemical air raid, and strapping her boots on, she lifted to the door, hoping in the Jeep renegade to intercept the outgoing convoy.

In the fields, the Frenchmen lay on the soft grass of Flanders, and Arya hummed the transistor to wake them. In the sky, the rouge light faded to the cerulean bleu of a spreading gas.

"Salut," she called out. "Est mal."

Within moments, a short range artillery shell floated across the sky, landing a hundred yards away. The blue gas seeped from the metallic alloy, rising in the early morning hours like a smoke, pirouetting into a dense fog.

"Ich nein haben vasser," a German artillery man said, lifting his hand to the air. "Ist dry."

Hoping out of her red renegade, Arya ran to a group of men lying in the Syrian air field, their limbs shaking uncontrollably. Pressing her hand against the German officer, she breathed into his lungs, gasping the air, and forcing it out as replaced her air mask to his.

"Ich sie gehen nerve gas," she replied. "Brauchen zwei."

Behind the chemical mask, the pale blue eyes of Caius looked to hers, and her sallow brow. Her eyes wore the dark mask and circle of a two week long deployment on four hours of sleep, but her grin had not faded.

His hand twitching, he reached up for her face, and she removed the mask, inhaling the air, and then releasing it and sucking the air from his lungs a second time.

"Moshten stand," she asked. "Ich nein sie aduye here."

Looking at her wrist, he noticed the sear of an open wound, and placed a tear of his sleeve over it.

"Cover ist," he said. "It will glow and bubble."

Arya grinned, and removed the air mask for a third time, inhaling and replacing it to his face. She pulled his arm over her shoulder, and lifted him to her back. Beneath his brust, he could feel the massive span of her back coursing into his, and as his hand shook, she placed it closer to her heart that he could feel her pulse.

On his finger tips, he could sense it pulsing hard, and he looked to the shallow stream across the field.

"Der," he said pointing. "Francois…ich sie haben aire libre auf die vasser."

Lowering into the stream, the pair intook a breath of air, and forced it out of their lungs.

"Is it water activated?" she asked in her second mask that she retrieved from the pool of dead on the stream bed.

"Nie, just force the air out, and lower and replace the clear air on top of the water to the field mask and short tank," he said, as the nerve endings in his hands began to feel again.

Overhead, the low lull of a medic E-VAC hovered, and Arya looked across the topography as droves ran from the chemical ground to the waiting chopper. She looked to Caius and pointed to the field house on the opposite side of the wood.

"Wir haben muerte," she said, looking at a drove of infantry with field packs and metallic canisters walking across the field kicking over the Frenchmen laying in the ground. "Gaben zwei und kommen auf meine baum a die haus."

Lifting cautiously from the water, the grey cerulean cloth of the Italian gerl drifted to the lower lands of the French field outside Flanders. Following her, four men fell into line and rank, stepping cautiously across the under brumble.

Along the path, Caius ran into Miche gasping for air on the ground. Clenching his side, he looked up to the German officer and reached up his hand. He looked to Arya, wearing a gas mask.

"You better tell that demon not to come at me with its lung," he said, looking at the shaking hand beneath his drifting eyesight. The gold of a wedding band shone in the dim light. "I'm not learning to chemical train that way."

Leaning down, Arya lifted her mask and cupped her lips, making a kissy face.

"Donne toi moin," she said, and lifted him from the ground. "I'm fascinated by du."

Placing her air tank and mask to his face, she grinned and slapped him on the back.

"Du don't have to kissiere moi," she said. "Some like dat…others, non."

Wandering in the wood, the five watched as Arya lifted basil, parsley, and dill from the underbrush. Reaching the field haus, she handed a Russe dagger to Miche.

"Voudrais vous ais sup?" she said. "Cortar le lettuce et wir haben congilio."

From the deep wood, a cerulean cloth and figure emerged holding trois congilio, or rabbit, bound by rope at the ear.

"Ist die best," she said, patting his shoulder.

It was Caius, hauling a fresh hunt for dinner. Together, the comrades joked and laughed playing an Italian song on the radio box as the first Allied aircraft docked overhead. It was over, the courageous campaign to the Italian sea shore, and now, sitting in the French field haus, the six supped, making light of the true terror they had traveled through.

"It was a gude war, meine Aberdessen," Caius said, resting his arm on Arya's shoulder.

"Nie, I'm a piece of shit…I left you strapped to the first ballistic," she said.

He looked to his new shoes.

"Ya, but I did get an awesome new pair of door runner shoes out of it," he said.

Putting on his shoe over his sock with a hole in it, he grinned and pointed to the hellcat's landing outside.

"You ready to head home?" he asked.

"Ja," the multilinguist rogue spy said. "Which one, though?"

Laughing, Caius lifted his rifle to his shoulder and the six wandered outside and stepped to the first inbound convoy home, free from the reign of terror of the second World War.

"Until next time, meine aberdessen," Arya said, waving good bye to the Frenchman standing in the light of the door.

And, the steel whirlbird assailed to the distance with the moon lit night and cloud cover.

The Forest Rescue

In le soir, the forest branches swayed softly in the rising moonlight as Caius lifted his soft footsteps through the dark soil. Lifting his archer's hook, he aimed the gilted bow he had made along the muddy riverbanks of the river Seine in the winter. Wandering in and around the meandering stream, a pale stag sipped the cool water of the French countryside.

"Maybe I'm looking for something I can't have," Caius said, lowering the bow and watching the sacred stag wander forward into the underbrush of the forest.

In the distance, his ears perked as he heard the sound of leaves moving in the nearby forest. It was not the sound of a sniper, but the cumbersome boot of a storm patrol, and there were three sets circling around an overturned log.

Ducking down, his chartreuse hood covered his face in the shadow of the night. The trio were pointing to the muddy hollow of an overturned log, where a small child had hidden in the afternoon. Caius has first spotted her wandering along the riverbank and led her through the forest with tiny ribbons on the tree limbs.

Now, at least fifteen years later, and having hunted the same forest in the duration of the war, he could not understand why there would be another set of small footprint to the wood.

In their arms, the trio carried a small congilio, and he grinned. It was his comrades from the first World War. There was Severin with his furrowed brow kicking at the dust, and there was Marcellius, his toothy grin shining in the moonlight, and at last, a small figure the size of a small boy.

Lowering his combat hood and face mask, he lofted through the pasture grasses to the other side of the riverbank. Raising his hand with his palm open, he lowered his rifle, and the three looked over, nodding.

In the place of a third tall form, there was Arya, and she was smaller than a child.

"Gude, Gott, Kinden," Caius said, looking to her lithe frame. It was lither than a decade before, and looked like she hadn't eaten in a month or slept in a year.

"Da, zehn nein freundlich," she said, lifting her palm and forearm. On it, the red mar of a lightning bolt, and Caius placed a kuss to it.

"They put a damn lightning bolt on it trying to replace the original stem," she added.

Caius watched as she kicked at the muddy rocks and pointed to the hollow log. In his eye, her dark green eyes burned the brightest red as a small aircraft lofted overhead.

Reaching for her arm, he looked to her.

"Wo ist?" he asked.

She drew a face in the dirt, and cut her eyes back, cursing the red Irishman that had led her from the wood and to the enemy lines of a foreign encampment.

"Ist die grun," she said.

Caius hugged her, and looked it over.

"It's a cool one," he said. "Not as frightful as before."

Arya sneered as snot shot out her nose; her hand trembled a bit and she sipped a cup of ale from her pack. Walking over to the fenceline by the trio, she kicked over a hollow stump.

"Glow worm," she said.

Pointing to the canister hidden in the hollow log, the radioactive glow worms pulsed in the metallic light canister. Lifting one, the cerulean bleu earthworm dropped to the soil and began to dig.

Jumping up from the soil, Severin began stomping the ground to get away. Arya laughed as she opened her palm; inside, the glow worm rolled to a ball and released its toxin to her palm.

She lifted her camping gear.

"Kommen meine haus," she said. "Ich sie Machen snakes, too."

Lifting his arm and wrapping it around the field scout, Caius placed a kiss on her cheek.

"Does it still fire off the big one?" he asked.

Flipping her palm over, she laughed.

"Of course," she said. "Never touched the oculum…dumb idiots. They thought I was just for the yellow ribbons."

And, wandering to the field haus, Arya began skinning the rabbit for dinner and crisping the skin of the wild rabbit on the open burner in the moonlight. Laughing, the quartet sipped on ale, vodka, and a bit of burnt coffee from Adrian's field rations.

Tossing a pack of cards to the table, Calvin walked in and replaced his

"Du look like a glowing nematode," he said, slapping Arya's arse.

"Man, du asked that enough," she replied, kicking her fur lined boots to his knee cap.

"Fuck," he said, groaning as he grasped his knee.

Lowering her eye, Arya looked over to Calvin with the innocence of the Red Cross. Her hand trembling, she placed a series of crochet blankets to the table.

"Moshten a nurse, schondie," she said, as he eyed the billions of crochet stitches on each blanket. Arya's hand no longer trembled.

"Nein, luft," he said. "Just turn out the light once in a while."

On the window sill, a glass of glowing lightning bugs illuminated the old cabin by the wood.

The Archer

Accelerating in the forest, the afternoon air filled with an impermeable smoke of fire and haze. Below the tree line, the scorch trails of the fire hailstorm cascaded to the trees and stumps in slow spirals with red contrails.

Lifting his footwork quickly over the tree stumps, Caius accelerated like a limber newborn deer through the forest.

The smoke filled the air as he heard a series of trees fall from overhead.

CRASH.

Looking up, he watched as the lithe door runner of the hellcat fell from overhead. Running forward, he lifted his arms to the air as the lithe para marine fell into his arms.

Removing his air mask, he looked down. She was the color of soot and smoke, and the ash of the forest fire had marked her face. Placing his fingertip to her chin, he quickly examined the beauty. She was unconscious.

Overhead, the tree branches continued to torch to flames as the forest fire engulfed the coastal forest. Throwing the lithe paramarine into a rack over his head, he ran forward leaping over fallen debris and trees in the forest.

From behind, an arrow whizzed past his ear and he retracted a hand dagger from his wrist piece, snapping it backwards in the direction of the fired arrow.

Stepping into the shallow water of a creek running through the forest, Caius trenched through the moisture table as the flames continued to engulf the forest. Waking slightly from the water splashing in her face, Arya muttered something about Bastion and Serai from the forest.

"Just watch me navigate," he said to the lithe beauty waking up. "Sugar, just cover your face."

Placing her down on a stone by the creek, he lifted his wrist watch to his ear piece to check for a signal. There was a single pulse registering nearby.

"Kommen, schondie," he said. "Ich nein sie haben aberdessen."

Standing up, Arya shook her arms as her spine popped back into place.

"Gott, Luft," he said. "Du nein faltan…wo ist du schmerz?"

Ripping off her soot filled jacket, her lace brassiere was the color of rouge. A single cross glimmered in the dying firelight by the stream bed.

"Ich nein ein," she said, casting down an arrow to the creek before racing off in the distance.

Throwing her shirt up to the air, Caius chased after the lithe beauty.

"Where are you going, du?" he shouted, and waved his arms to the nearby encampment along the forest fire edge.

"Nein du," she said, her voice echoing down the ravine as she slid.

Her artillery gear grappled with the roots and dirt of the hillside, before she stood again, and regained her strength up a rocky escarpment. Laughing from the opposite side of the ravine, Caius pointed to the pair of snipers standing on the edge.

Pausing, Arya opened her palms. From her artillery wristlets, she fired a pair of darts up the escarpment. The darts whizzed past the ear of Ruske and Severin as they ducked down.

Zigzagging along the hillside, Arya accelerated through the forest and back to the flames of the burning wood.

"Nein du," Caius said, jumping down from a tree and wrapping his arms around her ankles. Baring her clenched teeth, Arya stomped at his fingertips coiled around her boots.

"Da, meine," she said, as she reached up to a large uprooted tree. Lifting her body and wrangling from his grasp, she quickly sprang up to the top of the hillside ravine.

"You could be my luck," he shouted. "I have your shoes."

Pausing, the door runner paramarine looked to his gray running shoes. She paused.

"Du Aberdessen auf Deutsch," she shouted back.

"Ja, schondie," he said. "Same team."

Stopping, she looked down the ravine as a net fell overhead. Ensnared, she covered her face as Jaune walked up. The leather bootstraps of his renegade boots closed in on her ankle. He looked at the shoes and then flipped over her wrist.

"Ich nein Aberdessen," he said.

The lightning bolt scar on her wrist signaled a tag. He pointed to Caius.

"Take her away," he said. "She is going to be followed."

Lifting the lithe beauty in the net, Caius wandered far into the wood and placed her in the field cabin from years before. Arya looked up to him, quizzing.

"Du haus," he said. "Nein, kommen auf meine...ever."

In the dim candlelight, Arya lifted up some of the field journals in the cabin and placed her mark to them. It was the first night of freedom from capture, but the bittersweet regret of losing every friend known.

Outside, Caius whispered.

"She was tagged to find the rest of the ones she used to know," he said to Ruske. "She will have to leave or we can not stay."

Ruske kicked at the dirt beneath their feet.

"Da, sie wissen," he said. "Ich meine faltan...she was picked up in Provencal and shipped through Berlin...she may know something we don't know."

"Or she just could be retrained," Caius replied. "And, not know who she is or was."

Falling asleep in the room, Caius looked at the field journals and the photos of the sky she had taken across the countryside. There were contrails of landing sites, and a single drawing of a snake coiled around a large cylinder.

"Wo ist dat?" he asked the sleepy gerl.

"Mader bomb," she said. "Biggest one in the country."

Laughing, he fizzled out the candle.

"Get some sleep, schondie," he replied. "Du nein kennen und wissen."

www.ingramcontent.com/pod-product-compliance
Ingram Content Group UK Ltd.
Pitfield, Milton Keynes, MK11 3LW, UK
UKHW041924190726
13854UKWH00003B/1434